SONNETS

AND

SHORTER POEMS

SONNETS

AND

SHORTER POEMS

Petrarch

Translated by David R. Slavitt

HARVARD UNIVERSITY PRESS

Cambridge, Massachusetts · London, England

2012

Poems 1, 7, 8, 12, and 15 first appeared in *Per Contra*, issues 23 and 24.

Library of Congress Cataloging-in-Publication Data

Petrarca, Francesco, 1304–1374.
  [Rime. Selections. English]
  Sonnets and shorter poems / Petrarch ; translated by David R. Slavitt.
    p. cm.
  Includes bibliographical references.
  ISBN 978-0-674-06216-0 (alk. paper)
  1. Petrarca, Francesco, 1304–1374—Translations into English. I. Slavitt,
David R., 1935–   II. Title.
    PQ4496.E23S58 2012
    851'.1—dc22   2011016127

For Janet

et del suo lume in cima
chi volar pensa, indarno spiega l'ale.

CONTENTS

TRANSLATOR'S PREFACE

Francesco Petrarca (1304–1374), whom we call simply Petrarch, was born in Arezzo, where his father, a Guelph and a friend and ally of Dante, had relocated after leaving Florence, which had banished Dante in 1302. In 1312 Ser Petracco moved the family to Carpentras, in Provence, near Avignon, and there Francesco and his brother Gherardo were raised and educated. Provence was the wellspring of vernacular European poetry, and we can suppose that Francesco's being close to the novelty and excitement of the Provençal troubadours was at least a part of his development as a writer. He may have disliked Avignon's extravagance and self-indulgence, but his access to the libraries of his patrons there also provided him with an introduction to the classical tradition and especially the work of Horace, Ovid, and Virgil. A significant intellectual resource for him was St. Augustine's *Confessions,* a copy of which Dionigi da Borgo San Sepulcro, an Augustinian monk, gave him in 1333 and which surely demonstrated for the young poet the possibilities of drama in the idea of the fallen world and the tension between opposing ideals. Then, and perhaps most important, we know that by 1333 he had found a manuscript of Propertius, which he copied out, and, while Petrarch's vision of love is quite different from that of Propertius, there are also important correspondences. Loves that are happy and lead to a comfortable and fulfilling life are not the subjects of great literature. For Propertius—as for Dante in La Vita Nuova and for Petrarch—it is the unsatisfying or unsatisfied love that is interesting, endlessly eliciting explanations, redefinitions, self-accusation, and the high drama of torment.

Assuming that she existed at all,* Petrarch first beheld Laura at Easter mass on April 6, 1327, in the church of Sainte-Claire d'Avignon when he was twenty-two. Although she died on Easter Sunday in 1348 of the plague, Petrarch's obsession with her continued for the rest of his life. He did not think of her as a kind of earthly angel, as Dante considered Beatrice. Petrarch's idealization was of an entirely worldly passion that became a habit of mind, a way of living, and a source of inspiration for an astonishing body of work. There are 366 poems in the Canzioniere—a poem for each day of the year plus a final prayer—and the vast majority of its poems (317) are in the sonnet form. I have retained the original numeration, which therefore shows gaps where the missing pieces would go.

Petrarch has been of greater influence on English literature than Dante, Boccaccio, Ariosto, or any of that nest of singing birds that was the glory of the Italian Renaissance. Sir Thomas Wyatt and Henry Howard, the Earl of Surrey, did translations or adaptations of Petrarch's poems during the reign of Henry VIII, and by Elizabeth's time Petrarch's way of looking at the world, in which any instant and any mental connection, observation, or mood can be the prompting of a short poem, had been adopted as natural not only by Shakespeare but

* See F. J. Jones's "Further Evidence of the Identity of Plutarch's Laura," *Italian Studies* 39 (1984): 27–46.

also by Sir Philip Sidney and all those other adept lyricists of that remarkable age.

If Petrarch did not invent the sonnet, he was surely the poet who gave it life and energy. He is to the sonnet what Haydn is to the symphony. Petrarch has a number of canzoni and longer poems, which are interesting and attractive, but it was the short pieces, the quick takes for which he had a special talent and which turned out to be so influential, that interested me and were what I wanted to bring into English—not only the sonnets but the ballatas and the madrigals as well.

There are some readers who think that less might have been more—that there is too much of a muchness here, with the poet's obsessive concentration on his love for Laura, in which, inevitably, there is no small degree of repetition. My view is that this is a central part of Petrarch's intention. As in most poetry, the message is not paramount or even especially important. The repetitive quality of the poems is a way of demanding a closer scrutiny of the formal, craftsmanly aspects of the poems. Their rhymes are not merely decorative but are organic parts of the poems, which function—as most formal poetry does—as hypnotic inductions. To convey at least some suggestion of this in English, I think rhyme is necessary in translating them, even if the rhymes require some slight departure from the literal meaning of some of the sentences.

I have taken further liberties, necessary because English is rhyme-poor compared to Italian. In the octaves, for instance, I have allowed myself a different and less demanding set of rhymes for the second quatrain, which Petrarch never does. His scheme is generally ABBA ABBA, while my versions, allowing me a little wiggle room, are ABBA CDDC. The feeling—for both the reader and certainly for the writer—remains one of constraint. The technical aspects of the poems ought to be enough to maintain the interest of most readers, but I think the narrow range of subjects (only occasionally he writes a poem mourning the death of a friend or on some other subject not related to Laura) invites a close scrutiny to his performances *qua* performances. I think of Freud's notion of "the narcissism of small differences," and I suspect that these variations on a theme engage our interest precisely because of their narrow range.

Ceci dit, it is also true that nobody is required to read these through at a single sitting. (Or, well, maybe the first time, to get the sense of the arc of these poems, that might not be a bad idea.) But poetry—good poetry, surely—should be experienced more than once. And the second or third encounter could be more random in order to explore the richness of these sonnets and other short poems, how they refer to one another, and how the small variations in tone, even of the same trope or image, can make significant differences. Think, perhaps, of a painter who keeps doing flowers or horses or plates of fruit. We realize very quickly that the subject is not the flowers, horses, and fruit but the paintings themselves, and this, I am sure, was at least a part of Petrarch's intention. I do not suggest that his obsession with Laura was irrelevant, but it was the occasion as well as the subject of this extraordinary achievement.

There will be other readers who complain that I haven't done enough, and may question my exclusion of the longer poems. Obviously, I gave this decision considerable thought, but to have included them would have been to lose the book's focus on Petrarch's amazing acuity with the glances of sonnets. The structure of a sonnet, particularly of a Petrarchan sonnet, is to start with an octave of statement and then turn to a sestet of revision or refinement (or, occasionally, even dissent). For Petrarch this was a particularly congenial arena. The long poems, in no way deplorable, are composed, constructed, and one can see their structural elements. This makes them fundamentally different. Shakespeare's "Venus and Adonis" and "The Rape of Lucrece" are fine pieces of work, but they are not the poems on which his reputation rests. This is the case, too, I believe, with Petrarch, who could think in verse with felicity, but whose voice seems, centuries later, most authentic and authoritative.

There are Zen painters who meditate for hours, then pick up a large mop-like brush and do a single stroke on the piece of paper before them. That almost ethereal suddenness is what Petrarch was so good at, and, really, what he is known for, and that signature flair is what I most fundamentally have tried to convey.

SONNETS

AND

SHORTER POEMS

1

You who hear the sound in these scattered rhymes
of my sighs and sobs and the beating of my heart
when, as a youth with more passion than art,
I began to sing, as young men do sometimes,

in various styles, arguing or pleading,
I beg your indulgence for my perseveration
of hopes and sadnesses that in alternation
have tortured me and left me broken and bleeding.

Now I've become a figure in a tale
that old folks tell with a chuckle, and my name
even provokes laughter. It isn't right.

Ambition tempts you, and you try and fail,
and reap bitter remorse instead of fame
for having chased a dream of the world's delight.

2

To accomplish a graceful act of revenge and in one
single day redress a thousand slights,
Love took up his bow and hid in the night's
shadows, biding his time for the opportune

moment in which to strike. I was defenseless
and although I had withstood many times before
his skirmishes and onslaughts in this war,
this time his arrowhead struck and I fell senseless.

Thus, undone at his first pass, my heart
could not rally its forces to defend
itself and prevent a rout and my overthrow.

Neither could it withdraw to some safe part
of the wood in which to hide and try to send
help for the pains it knew I would undergo.

3

It was on that day when the sun's bright rays fade
in pity for its maker's passion that I
was taken unprepared at the instant when my
eyes met yours and I was at once betrayed.

Good Friday wasn't a time to be protected
from Love's assaults, and consequently without
any prudence or caution, I wandered about
among the mourning crowd, sad and dejected.

Love found me unarmed and helpless; he
saw that my eyes were an easy way to my heart
(those passageways that so easily fill with tears).

What honor can he claim for taking part
in a one-sided battle he won by treachery
without the need for cannons, swords, or spears?

4

How infinite the providence and the art
He showed us in his creation's manifold
wonders in which great contrarieties hold
together, despite the forces that pull them apart.

He descended to earth to illuminate the script
in which the truth was written, could we but read,
and to take the nets from John and Peter and lead
them to fish for men's souls thus equipped.

He could, had he chosen, have been born in Rome
but he picked Judea for its humility
that was what we would expect him to prefer

and in a village there, wise men could see
a bright sun rise. That such things can occur
makes proud this world that is my Lady's home.

5

When my desperate sighs call out the name
Love has inscribed on my heart, the very first
audible and significant sound to burst
forth is "LAU," a syllable the same

as that of her cognomen. With "RA" next,
the not quite random phonemes take on meaning,
so that I am no longer merely keening
but signifying now with a lovely text.

It is not me but speech itself that calls
out to LAUd your RAdiant grace and bask
in the rich shimmer that from your person falls.

Apollo raises an eyebrow here: it galls
him that a mortal is equal to the task
of such song that both celebrates and enthralls.

6

My passion's folly is such that it runs
after whatever flees from Love's lasso
as certain sporting dogs are seen to do:
any slight movement seizes it at once.

I try to call it back, but it ignores
my whistles and commands, preferring its own
instincts to my training, and all alone
scampers ahead in a way its master deplores.

Indeed, I am the one to take commands
rather than give them, and after my passion goes
my will, toward the ruin I can well foresee.

In the depths of the glade he has led me to, there stands
the laurel, prized but bitter, heaven knows,
and it does not offer any solace to me.

7

Avarice and excessive indolence in
our comfy beds have turned our natures bad,
corrupting them and making us a sad
mockery of what we could have been.

Heaven's lights are dimmed: all dreams of glory
seem in our time to have somehow guttered out
or given way to sloth and the spirit's doubt
so that Helicon's spring is dismissed as a children's story.

Laurel and myrtle? What earthly use are they?
Philosophy wanders about, naked and poor,
while practical men seek comforts that gold buys.

The path you have chosen is arduous and obscure,
but do not, gentle spirit, turn away
on that account from your noble enterprise.

8

At the foot of that green hill where we once flew
free as the air, in a small cage we now sing
and we awaken you and therefore bring
you to that sleeplessness he struggles through

whose gift we were. Now he, and you, and we
suffer together at cruel Love's behest,
all held captive who were lately blessed
with the joy of going our ways, untrammeled and free.

Our prospects may be grim but there is release
that death gives to all creatures, soon or late,
when even our tiny souls may find some peace

in understanding that our captor's fate
will be much more severe than ours, for he's
Love's captive: his unending torments are great.

9

When the stars and planets that tell the hour arrive
at the house of Taurus, power from those burning
horns pours down to clothe the world, returning
its springtime colors, vivid and alive.

Verdant meadows and hillsides, resplendent in May
with buds and flowers, dazzle us awake
whose minds had been dulled by winter, and we take
delight in the fecundity on display.

Fruits on the boughs of trees will ripen and grow,
ready to be gathered while she, like the sun
among the ladies, turning her eyes toward me

will engender in me a springtime longing that none
but she can satisfy. From her *yes* or *no*
my summer's warmth will come, or frigidity.

10

Glorious Colonna,* in you are all
our hopes, for your great colonnade withstands
the bolts that come from Jupiter's angry hands
and through his worst storms stands firm and tall,

raising our intellects from earth to the high
heaven, and not in imposing edifices
but *en plein air* on the green meadow, and this is
where poetry is born beneath the sky.

All day birds trilled and at night the nightingale
sang sweetly so in daylight or in shade
our hearts were serenaded. Now alone

we are bereft. The music, I am afraid,
continues still, but in a minor scale,
as we listen to it, sad that you are gone.

---

* Stefano Colonna, whose son, Cardinal Giovanni, was Petrarch's patron.

11[*]

Neither in the sun's glare nor in the shade
do you remove your veil, because you know
what it would do to me, so
in love am I that you are half afraid.

When, in my dejection, I desired to die,
I glimpsed your face, radiant with compassion,
but the fierce love that it inspired within me
frightened you, and you adopted the fashion
of wearing a veil. This was the reason why
you hid your features in its obscurity
and took away what I most wanted to see.
So that I am musing
once more on death—a subject not of my choosing
but of my hopes that were raised and are betrayed.

---

* A ballata, which is a variation on the sonnet form, with the third and
twelfth lines shorter.

12

My life of sighs and bitter tears could be made
even more difficult and more absurd
if I were to see the face I once preferred
to every other grown old and decayed,

the eyes dimmed and the hair that once was gold
changed to silver, the posies laid aside,
and forgotten (except by me). I am sure that I'd
shed new tears more copious than the old.

But then Love might at last give me confidence
to speak to you and explain clearly how
through all those days and years with an intense

passion I have loved you. Even allow
for the passage of time: it has made no difference,
except that I've grown used to love's pains now.

13

From time to time, on other ladies' faces
there may be sparks of love that strike in me
a response, although it is less ardent than she
produces in my heart, and on that basis

I offer thanks for the moment when I was given
the honor beyond my merit to behold
her striking beauty, worthy of the cold
empyrean heights one might expect in heaven.

From her come loving thoughts of the kind that lead
to noble and virtuous actions that one would
associate with grace. She makes me good,

redeems me from the passions of the blood,
and draws me up. Miraculously freed
from gravity's drag, to heaven I proceed.

14*

O weary eyes, without my agreement turning
toward that gorgeous face that you know will slay
me, exercise caution, I pray,
for I am already sick with love and yearning

to which only Death can offer any end
by closing off the avenue that leads
to that sweet portal on which my mind is fixed
in an appetite that grows the more it feeds
upon that vision. You can be my friend
and save me—and yourselves as well, for you
are mortal meat that must in the end come to
the nothingness, which may be
not so far off, if you could only see
through all our tears the blackness's vivid burning.

---

* Another ballata.

15

At every dragging step I am able to take
with my weary body racked with constant pain,
the image of your face that I keep in my brain
gives me the courage and will to bear the ache.

But I ask myself why do I go so far
on this long road in this brief life and I pause
to look down at the dust and weep because
I separate myself from where you are.

How, I ask myself, can I endure
this way with my limbs and spirit cut apart
from one another? And Love, who always hovers

nearby, answers: "Do not be faint of heart:
the distance will not kill you, you may be sure,
for this is the special privilege of lovers."

16

His hair grizzled, the old man says his good-byes
to the mournful wife and children he leaves at home,
determined to make a pilgrimage to Rome
and see its holy places before he dies.

His desire is such that he drags his weary bones
along the road by the pure strength of his will
and the dream he is determined to fulfill
as he struggles past the challenging milestones.

At last he arrives and gazes at marble or paint
of the face of him he hopes to see again later
in heaven above. I compare his devout

joy to my hopes that do not fail or faint
of seeing faces that can suggest your greater
beauty I think of always and dream about.

17

In bitter rivulets tears run down my cheeks
and with them the winds of sighs I cannot prevent
whenever I behold your face, which has meant
hopelessness to my soul in what it seeks.

Your gentle smile calms my fiery passion
and spares me the torment that I undergo
so much of the time, for when you are near I know
a higher joy and contentment after a fashion.

But then you turn away and I remain
behind in the dismal cold of the stars set
in the dark vastness that I know bode me ill.

My spirit quits my body then, not yet
satisfied, and follows in your train,
leaving me with neither brain nor will.

18

When I have turned my eyes toward my Lady's face
I am blinded as if by the shine of a light so bright
that broad daylight is dazzled into night
and I have no sense either of time or place.

I feel my body melting and my mind
and heart abandon what remains of me
that gropes as best it can toward entropy,
undone by the cruel glare of this rare kind.

My impulse is to flee these heavy blows
but how can I when my desire comes, too,
as rapidly as I can go, my own

shadow? I am reluctant to disclose
my misery to the world. All I want to do
is weep my bitter tears and be left alone.

19

Some creatures in the world have eagle eyes
that can see even in the bright glare of the sun,
while others are different and therefore have to shun
daylight and only forage beneath dark skies.

Still others, we know, are drawn to the brightness of fire
but do not understand that it also burns.
I am like them, afraid and eager by turns
as natural caution struggles with my desire.

I am not strong enough to look at her face
nor clever enough to hide myself away
from her daylong dazzle. Like some helpless bug

I am drawn to the light, although I know that way
sure ruin waits. Helpless, in utter dismay
I contemplate my fate with a stoic shrug.

20

I am ashamed that I have been so long
silent about your phenomenal beauty, which should
have prompted me to produce a poem that could
at least have tried to describe it in sweet song.

But I find that my wit is insufficient. The task
is daunting, and the more I cogitate
the less I feel equipped for such a great
performance as the circumstances ask.

Many times I have cleared my throat to speak
but no words poured forth to do what I had willed
as if I'd been struck dumb by the enterprise.

I've even written a line or two, but weak,
inadequate, and clumsy—and I was stilled
after the signal failure of many tries.

21

A thousand times, dear adversary, have I
offered you my heart in the hope of peace
but you reject a gift that fails to please
a fastidious taste I cannot satisfy.

And if some other lady were to pursue
this heart, her hopes of winning it would be vain,
for she could never counter the disdain
I feel for it myself, because of you.

I banish my heart and altogether disown
a uselessness that cannot look for aid
from you either. Let it go its way.

What mischief it may get into I'm afraid
I cannot guess as it wanders on its own,
having lost you, its anchor and mainstay.

24

Had not the laurel tree, which is said to be
immune to the bolts of Jove, refused to give
her wreath to my poor brow (because I live
devoting myself to the art of poetry),

I would be a grateful friend to the Muses
from whom this benighted age has turned away.
Where are Minerva's laureates today?
Where are the poems our generation produces?

The Ethiopian sands cannot burn with more
heat than the fire that rages within my
soul having lost what I most adore.

Helicon's sacred fountain is nowhere nearby
but only that of the bitter tears that pour
in a mockery I need not amplify.

25

Love used to weep and I would be weeping, too,
because I was so often with him—and I
saw how your brave soul after many a try
freed itself from his snares as few men do.

Now with the help of God it is on the true
path, ascending steadily, with my
admiration and thanks for the mercy by
which this signal success has come to you.

If in this restoration to the right
road, you have been disrupted by hedgerows
and steep hills and have found the going rough,

it is a demonstration, heaven knows,
of difficulties surmounted from which men might
take courage if they have the will and faith enough.

26

No ship that came to harbor at last, storm-tossed
and tumbled by the mad waves' violent whims
where the passengers gave thanks in prayers and hymns,
amazed that they and the ship had not been lost,

occasioned such delight and relief in me.
No prisoner condemned but then set loose
from the rough embrace of the rope of the hangman's noose
could cause in me the joy I feel to see

how in your battle Love has put away
his sword to end his fight and yield to my lord.
We who write about Love are hard put to say

how splendid this is. In their celestial concord
the angels care more for one who had gone astray
than the ninety and nine with whom they are slightly bored.

27

Philip VI, who inherited Charlemagne's crown
has taken arms to break proud Baghdad's horns
and vanquish Islam which his people scorns.
Christ's vicar, Benedict, in tiara and gown,

holding the holy keys, is going home
and barring any misadventure he
will pass through Bologna and very soon will be
back in the Vatican in noble Rome.

The lambs fight with the wolves in sordid actions
prompted by ambition and greed that tears
towns apart as these competing factions

savage each other during these dismal years.
Rome is not well served by such distractions
as the time to fight against the Moslems nears.

31

The gentle soul that threatens to depart,
called to the afterlife so prematurely
will have earned a place of honor surely,
in the choicest precincts of the heavens' chart.

If she should stay between Venus and Mars,
the Sun itself would be dimmed, for every eye
would turn toward her in order to descry
this new light that has come among the stars;

if she should be placed below the Sun's
fourth sphere, then Venus, Mars, and even the Moon
will find themselves in shadow all at once;

or, if in the fifth, then she will soon
ascend to the orbit in which Jupiter runs,
dimming all the stars as if it were noon.

32

The closer I come to my last day that must
eradicate my pains and assuage my woes,
the more clearly I see how fast Time goes
and that my hopes in him will turn to dust.

I tell myself that in only a while all these
pratings about love that occupy
my days will come to an end, and if I sigh
it will be in relief as I find peace and ease.

Along with the clay my hopes, too, will expire
that made me speak so wildly and for so long
as the gusts of rage and torrents of tears abate.

My illusions and mankind's have been wrong
that so often goad us in our blind desire
to sorrows that we later repudiate.

33

Already in the east, bright Venus gleamed
and off in the north, Calisto and Arcas spun
where Juno had put them for what Jove had done,
and men who were still in bed dreamed that they dreamed.

Old servants, barefoot, fanned the slumbering fires
and lovers felt the shared pangs of their sorrow
that darkness had given way to the careless morrow
and that they had to rise from their night's desires.

It was then that my enfeebled hopes returned
to vex my heart from my dreams or, say, nightmares
for I could feel real tears upon my face.

She was different now, burdened by age and cares,
and as she mocked me, her eyes that I loved burned:
"You may yet see me again, somehow, someplace."

34

Apollo, if the desire that drove you once
into the woods after that girl with the gold
hair and if the blood has not turned cold
that yet in the vessels of your body runs,

protect from icy wind and numbing frost
those twigs and fronds in which we both were snared
by Love in a catastrophe we shared,
for otherwise my hopes are surely lost.

Will you not for love's sake clear the air
of these obscuring fogs and mists so we
can both behold the sight of my Lady's face

as she sits on a blanket on the grass somewhere
and shades her eyes from the sunlight? We will see
a nonpareil of loveliness and grace.

35

Pensive, alone, I wander deserted fields
with hesitating steps, glancing this way
and that, my eyes peeled for any stray
signs of human life the landscape yields.

This is the only way I know to defend
against the condescension of those who can see
the misery in my bearing and pity me
for the anguish burning within me without end.

I yearn for wild seashores, deep woods, and such
congenial places where no human has ever
ventured and where my soul in these byways

can find some peace in solitude. But much
more persistent than I had imagined and clever,
Love dogs my footsteps, arguing his case.

36

If I could believe that death would bring release
from the amorous obsessions that occupy
my mind, I would resort to those measures by
which I could end these irksome fantasies,

But what if dying only changes me
from present torments to others even worse
that my difficulties now mildly precurse
and my poor spirit never can be free?

High time, however, for that remorseless bowman
to loose his arrow already soaked with blood
at me, for I am his and swear that no man

was ever more deeply wounded in this wood.
As hunters do with game, she with this human
prize should end my agonies for good.

38

Orso, my friend, there never was a brook
or hill or wall or leafy branch overhead
that blocked the sunshine or a cloud that spread
itself across the sky from which I took

umbrage or complained, but the thing that hides
those lovely eyes of hers from my hungering view
I cannot bear, her veil that tells me to
go off somewhere to weep and mocks and derides.

That gaze she lowers in a show of modesty
destroys my spirit. It is as if she were
preparing me to hear my obsequy

before my time. I also complain of her
delicate hand, so quick to do to me
the hurts I'd expect from a hardened torturer.

39

I am assailed by those fair eyes in which
Love and Death reside to threaten me.
I am transfixed although I wish to flee
as a boy might who is threatened with a switch.

No place can be too difficult of access
for me to attempt to find some refuge where
I can be safe from her sweet basilisk stare,
which reduces me to utter senselessness.

If I have been dilatory in visiting you,
my friend, understand it is only because I fear
encountering her who makes me suffer like this.

To return at all to the place where she is near
requires courage of me, and if you knew
how much, you'd see how true my friendship is.

40

If Love and Death do not between them shred
the fabric I am fashioning here and, free
of sticky birdlime spread out on the tree,
I can escape to soar with my wings spread,

joining truth with truth in the modern style
but with ancient speech for something doubly good,
as I have the brashness to suppose I could,
I shall delight all Rome and make you smile.

But I am short of some of the thread I need
if I am to finish this great project of mine
(even father Livy needed to eat).

I ask for your patronage for my design
that has until now supported me. I plead
for the sake of the work you'll approve when it's complete.

41

When that laurel tree Apollo loved is gone
from its rightful place in the forest, Vulcan begins
to fashion mighty thunderbolts for the sins
that have angered Jove, who wants to hurl them down

in Janus's month or Julius Caesar's—for rage
knows no season. The earth weeps, and the sun
hides itself from what is being done
by the heavenly gods upon the earthly stage.

Saturn's boldness returns and the wrath of Mars
that bring us storms; Orion stirs the seas
to wreck the tillers of ships and break their spars.

Aeolus shows Juno and Neptune that he's
infuriated, and showers of falling stars
mark her departure and the world's decrease.

42

That sweet and gentle smile of hers is gone,
one of the earth's great glories, and now in vain
under Aetna Vulcan need not strain
with the hammer and the anvil he bangs on.

Jove has no need anymore for those bolts he throws
and his gentle sister Latona reawakes
to a more congenial planet Apollo takes
delight in, while a gentle zephyr blows.

Sailors are now secure and have no need
of courage or skill, as if behind them there were
a wake only of meadow flowers. Indeed,

all stars of evil omen have fled or defer
to her fair face as now we all proceed
into a better time we owe to her.

43

Nine times had Latona's son peered down from his high
balcony in search of the one for whom
he'd sighed and felt the iterative boom
of his heart but now was embraced and desired by

another. No matter how closely he scanned
the landscape, he failed to find the faintest trace
near or far of her so yearned-for face
and he felt great grief and was a god unmanned.

He never again glimpsed the features that I
shall praise, if I live, for a thousand pages or more,
for along with him, I am afflicted by

her absence, devastated and heart sore.
At the end, she wept tears that will never die
but perfume the air with the sweetness it had before.

44

Caesar, who was quite prepared to turn
Thessaly into a wasteland of ashes and blood,
sat down to weep for fallen Pompey, his good
friend and son-in-law. He could discern

the features on the severed head they'd brought.
David, who killed Goliath, was undone
by the death of Absalom, his beloved son,
and by the death of Saul he was distraught.

But you never feel the slightest pity for my
suffering who are armed against Love's bow
that he has drawn against you but always in vain.

You see me on the rack enduring slow
torments but shed no tear and sigh no sigh
and only sneer in scorn at your friend's pain.

45

My adversary, the one in whom she sees
those eyes gaze on the face that I adore,
a doubled vision in the glass before
which she stands, a pair of effigies

of beauty itself! By attending thus to him,
you drive me from the place where I desire
to be, however unworthy (if I aspire
to reflect you that way, I know my hopes are dim).

If only I were nailed up on your wall,
better than your mirror, I would reflect
you correctly, full face and either side.

You'd be less stern and arrogant, and above all
less vain. If Narcissus' story is correct,
there's peril in such self-absorption and pride.

46

Like a spendthrift's gold and pearls, the summer's red
and white flowers soon wither away
leaving only their thorns behind, and they
wound me: I am wholly discomfited.

So my days drag along in tears and woe
with a grief that is ever refreshed and always new
for which I blame those damnable mirrors you
look into often, confirming what you know.

How can Love persuade you to my side
when you are so absorbed in your image where
all your desires happily abide?

It is a hellish condition. The waters there
make you forget the world. Unsatisfied,
I languish in hopelessness and black despair.

47

I feel the spirits within me guttering out
that are nourished not so much by you as by hope,
but all mortals decline along a slope
steep or gentle—its end is not in doubt.

Why then should I rein in my desire
in order to survive? Better to be
honest and let my passions run wild and free
wherever they will, although the risk is higher.

Let it lead me back to those splendid eyes
from which I shrink in order not to be
an annoyance and risk the dangers Love defies.

A single glance from them would provide for me
fulfillment. How many men can realize
their fondest dream and then die happily?

48

Fire never put out a fire and rain
never dried out a riverbed—but we know
that while like increases with like, it is also so
that oppositions can foster some kinds of gain.

Love dominates our thoughts and by him our two
bodies contrive to sustain a single soul.
But why, if this is the case, should it be his goal
to diminish desire as a surplus seems to do?

As the upper Nile deafens with the sound
of its mighty falls, as the sun's brightness can blind
those who stare into it, so, too, with desire

in discord with itself in a troubled mind.
Spurred on too much, it balks and turns around
and flees in fear from the heat of its own fire.

49

Ungrateful tongue, I have tried as well as I could
to keep you from telling lies, and I have done
honor to your achievement, but you have won
no honor for me or brought me any good.

I call upon you to help me as I utter
my pleas for mercy, but you are cold and dumb
and, if you speak at all, it is in some
pathetic gibberish someone asleep might mutter.

And you, you mournful tears, are with me here
at night when I should rather be alone,
but then when daylight comes you always flee.

And you, my sighs, as heavy as if a stone
were on my chest, you also disappear,
so that only my face tells the truth about me.

51

If the dazzle had come closer to my eyes
that even at a distance shattered me
then, as it happened once in Thessaly,
I'd have assumed an entirely different guise.

But what new metamorphosis could make
me any more hers than I am now?
Perhaps I could become a stone somehow
on which her name is chiseled for love's sake,

adamant, perhaps, or marble—white
with fear—or else rock crystal that men admire.
At any rate, the weight I can barely stand

to carry of my burden of desire
would lift: I envy Atlas with his light
load of the sky in Morocco's burning sand.

52*

Diana herself could not have been more pleasing
to Actaeon when he saw her in the blue
water of the pond that was close to freezing

than that shepherdess was whom I once happened to
see washing her gauzy veil in a brook.
She smoothed her hair because of a breeze that blew,

and although the sun was blazing down, I took
a sudden chill and my whole body shook.

---

* A madrigal.

54[*]

It was because of her irresistible face
that my foolish heart was prompted to follow, for she
seemed beyond compare in beauty and grace.

But along the way, as I passed through a green valley,
I heard a voice from a distance telling me,
"You are wasting your time. You must not dilly-dally."

I paused in the shade of a huge beech tree where I gazed
in all directions and thought of the great danger
that lurked in these woods. Above, the noon sun blazed

as I turned back from this mad pursuit of a stranger.

---

[*] A madrigal.

55*

That fire within me I had thought cruel time
and the coming on of age had quenched now flares
up again, taking me unawares.

It hadn't died, although there were no more
sparks or tongues of flame but there was heat
underneath the ashes, waiting for
its moment to revive, and my defeat
this time could be worse and more nearly complete.
Tears well again as in these sorry affairs
they often do, distilled from my griefs and cares.

One might suppose that such a flood would be
enough to quench any flames that it came near,
but Love has decided on opposite torments for me
to delude me so that what might at first appear
to be an escape is only the trap I fear
snapping more firmly shut as it prepares
to bind me even more tightly in its snares.

---

* A ballata.

56

In utter folly, I have been counting the hours
assuming that if I could somehow endure
long enough, then I could be sure
of success—but the sweetness of my waiting sours.

There is no harvest; the seed declines to sprout;
a predator is ravaging my sheepfold.
I wait for springtime's warmth, but still it is cold.
Time passes, and my hopes are giving out.

I do not know, but I begin to dread
that I have been duped by Love, and hope for joy
never comes except to fill my head

with dreams that try my soul. Who has not read
the words I learned when I was just a boy:
no man can be called happy until he is dead?

57

My ventures are too complicated and slow
and my hopes rise only to fall again,
exhausting first my faith in them and then
my patience, which abandon me and go.

It's madness: snowdrifts will sooner be warm and black,
the sea waveless, the fish frisk on the high
Alpine peaks, and the sun will decline in the sky
to set in the east and follow a new track

than I will find some equipoise and peace
or Love and my Lady cease to conspire together
for amusement to torture me and to maltreat

their captive. Sometimes there is a change in the weather
but only after much bitterness are these
rare moments, tainted and bittersweet.

58*

I send a pillow on which your cheek may find
some rest and solace after all that weeping
because the god you follow has been keeping
you from repose in body and in mind.

And the book is to block the left-hand road from where
Love's couriers come with offers and blandishments.
One learns in time to cope with such events
in winter's cold or summer's balmy air.

My third cadeau is a tisane that you may
find soothing (it is sour but then turns sweet).
And then there's this little sonnet, which I pray

may keep my name alive so that someday
after my life has ended and I meet
Charon, its echo will not fade away.

---

* Probably sent to Agapito Colonna.

59[*]

Although the fault of another has freed me from
Love's initial snares
I am not extricated from these affairs.

Among those golden locks Love had concealed
his line of insidious traps
and from those cold eyes came glances that congealed
my heart in which there was a total lapse
of thought and in these gaps
my soul forgot all other earthly cares
or hope of heaven in my fervent prayers.

And then those flashing eyes were taken away
that I had gazed into
and those lovely tresses . . . I cannot convey
my grief that they were gone, too.
No fear of Death can possibly undo
my longing for her. My memory still bears
the sight of breezes tousling her stray hairs.

---

[*] A ballata.

60

The noble tree that I have for so long
loved and in its shade in idle hours
have learned to bring forth with my feeble powers
strains from time to time of acceptable song

has changed, and its soft wood has now become
harder than iron so that the only string
left in my lyre is love. I cannot sing
of anything else, but I find I am stricken dumb.

My early rhymes, more cheerful, looked on life
with hopes but the one I loved has dashed all these
and my heart is leaden and I am undone.

Let poets who are sitting under trees
where lovers have carved their initials with a knife
see their leaves curl and die in the heat of the sun.

61

Blest be the day, the month, the year's season,
the hour, the very instant of the clock
when I was caught, stupefied by the shock
of seeing those eyes that robbed me of all reason.

And blest be that first constriction of my chest
in a breathlessness they must know in paradise
as I was seized by Love, for in a trice
I felt his arrow strike deep in my breast.

Blest be the many words that came from me
invoking her name, and blest, too, be the sighs
of my passion and my many tears. Blest be

the pages in the pile that I've watched rise
and that purchased for her a certain celebrity,
for the world now sees her with my loving eyes.

62

Father in heaven, many a day and night
have I tossed in sleeplessness, the raging fire
blazing in my heart of my desire
for her in whose grace I took such delight.

From now on, though, I pray that my heart and mind
may be inspired by you to a better way
of living, the adversary kept at bay,
and that in your fire I may be refined.

For eleven years I have been in her thrall,
hopeless, helpless, worthless, but on this
Good Friday, I resolve to make good my loss.

Miserere, let your sweet pity fall
upon my head. To a better place than this,
lead me, Lord, who suffered on the cross.

63[*]

Your lovely eyes noticed my pallor, more
severe than ever, suggesting that I must be near
death, and compassion moved you, if not fear,
to greet me, revive my hopes, and thus restore

the fragile life that still remained in me,
which is the gift of your eyes and voice, so that all
I am I owe to them and the gentleness
of your gesture that you might have thought was small.

As the herdsman with his switch occasionally
prods lazy beasts, you in your tenderness
aroused in my heart the new life I possess.

This then and my heart I owe to you
and I go forth in a fair fresh wind with new
hopes, a different man than I was before.

---

[*] A ballata.

64

If you had been different in your behavior, more deft
in avoiding my longing glances, more demure
in the way you held your head up and let your
smile dazzle the world, if you had left

the room a moment before or turned aside,
and you had not made an imprint on my life
where the laurel branches of Love are growing rife,
then your disdain might be well justified.

No plant should have to grow in such dry soil,
and I understand that you might choose to be
elsewhere on ground that you would find better suited,

but since, on the whim of fate you have found in me
a habitat, I urge you not to recoil,
but learn like a plant to thrive where you are rooted.

65

Alas, I had no fear on that first day
when Love declared himself with a wily attack,
taking two steps forward and then one back
in order not to alarm me in any way.

But the bars of my stubborn heart could not resist
the repeated strokes of his destructive rasp,
and soon I found myself within his grasp,
wits gone, will gone, a docile fatalist.

There are no defenses left for me to try
except to beg for whatever mercy he
may be inclined to show to mortals. I

do not expect him to listen—except that she
may also be so stricken that this fire in my
breast may rage in hers as well for me.

67

Up on the Tyrrhenian seashore
where the weeping waves are broken by the breeze,
I saw the lofty boughs of the laurel trees
of which I have written and will write even more.

Love had been seething in my soul to impel
with recollections of that soft blonde hair
my celebration, and by a small brook there
I tumbled down, as if in a fainting spell.

What I felt was shame, for what kind of man is this
who so easily gives way to a pretty place
and feels his heart stirring within and his

spirit on fire? It should not be the case
that any external prompting from nature is
needed, with my feet as wet as my face.

68

At the prospect of the holy city, I feel
deep shame for my misdeeds and my many grave
sins: I chide myself and resolve to save
myself, and my desire to change is real.

But another thought pops into my mind—of how
I might go back to my Lady and gaze at her,
which is a thing to do that I prefer
above all else. Why not return home now?

I feel a chill as I realize how light
and fickle is my mind and changeable. No
sooner have I decided what is right

than the opposite notion beckons to me to go
to seek the life of pleasure and appetite
and I vacillate in an endless to-and-fro.

69

I know perfectly well that sensible plans
from intelligent people never do any good
in struggles with you, who with your many shrewd
tricks can entrap your victims, and no man's

defenses are worth a damn. I've run away
from Love and gone to sea where the dangers might
clear my head and help me in this fight
and the fresh winds and the tang of the salt sea spray.

From your clutches, Love, I escaped at least for a while,
lived from moment to moment, tossed by the waves,
and breathed freely, but by your craft and guile

your messengers found me out, those crafty knaves
who lurked in the lee of one of those distant isles,
to claim me as masters do their runaway slaves.

74

My thoughts of you are unwearied, even though
I am exhausted by them and wish I could flee
from this grievous load of sighs that burdens me
and find some other life to which I could go.

All this perseveration about your face,
your hair, and your lovely eyes about which I
go on continually, with my tongue and my
voice, is absurd. I am helpless, a mental case.

My feet are relentless that follow in your footprints
and both of us are embarrassed, as I am aware.
That it's pointless, I know: you do not need to convince

or chastise me. I sit here in my chair
writing of you, although it makes you wince.
But it's not my fault: it's Love's doing, I swear.

75

My wound from those lovely eyes is very grave
but nothing else can restore my strength to me.
Soothing herbs or healing stones from the sea
or the charms that witches mutter sometimes to save

the afflicted cannot help me. Not even the fond
glances of any other woman can do
a thing for me. I think only of you,
for I know my malady is far beyond

another's cure. Love's arsenal has no need
for other or better weapons than these to achieve
an utter rout, and I capitulate,

acknowledging my defeat. But it can relieve
me to speak of those eyes. As my words proceed
haltingly, I feel my pains abate.

76

Love with his fawning and empty promises
has brought me back to my old prison cell
and has given the keys to her who is my fell
foe. I was foolish once again and this is

humiliating, but I shall yet contrive
my freedom with my sighs and I shall seize
and break the chains I wear through strategies
I have prepared beforehand. I shall survive

by winning her pity. My pallid face and brow
that make it seem that I am at death's door
will soften her heart and speak for me somehow.

Her heart is not hard enough to stand before
my distressing visage and to allow
the suffering that gentle women deplore.

77

If Polyclitus or any of his peers
in Greek sculpture looked for such a one
as to equal my Lady's beauty, they'd find none,
not even if they searched for a thousand years.

But surely my Simone* must have been
in heaven when he captured on a sheet
of paper Laura's features that would defeat
any earthly artist's brush or pen,

for here the body often veils the soul
disfiguring the perfection in which it came
from heaven, and to capture which was his goal,

as well as to bring both her and him great fame,
braving the heat and cold here to extol
a face with a perfection heaven could claim.

---

* Simone Martini, who must have painted Laura's portrait.

78

To please me, Simone took his pencil and
drew her face, but had he given his
image voice and intellect, then this
would be astounding from any human hand

and all my piteous sighs would disappear.
If what he drew, so lovely and so meek,
and full of peace were only able to speak,
she would surpass any other beauty here

on earth. Pygmalion prayed for the dispensation
that I imagine and by which I could hold
with the artist's work a single conversation,

for if from Pygmalion's astonishing creation
this was the outcome, as we have been told,
why can't I dream of a similar transformation?

79

If the beginning, fourteen years ago,
of this long road of sighs had held any slight
clue of what would follow or if I might
have guessed what degree of suffering I would know

from Love, under whose harsh yoke I live,
with no relenting, would I have turned away
my eyes from what destroys me? I cannot say.
But I struggle on from day to day and give

no hint of how I weaken. No one but me
suspects how her briefest glance can melt my heart.
My soul has managed to come this far but I fear

I cannot last much longer, and I start
to worry that death is waiting, for I can see
its shadow looming larger as it comes near.

81

I am exhausted by this load I bear
of heavy sins and this wicked way of living
and fear I am lost and there is no forgiving
for what I have done: I am in despair

and my enemy laughs. But I have a great friend
who came to save me with grace and courtesy.
Then he took flight, and the face was lost to me
of him on whom I had come to depend,

but I hear his voice resounding here below:
"O you who labor, I can set you free
unless someone bars the path you should take."

What love, what mercy or destiny can there be
to let me acquire the wings of a dove and go
high up to follow him for goodness' sake?

82

I have never wearied, my Lady, of loving you,
nor shall I do so as long as I live, but I
have reached the sorry end of my tether, and my
endless weeping disgusts me (and you, too).

I should prefer to go to a simple grave
than a fancy tomb on which is carved your name
when my spirit is redeemed from the flesh's claim
and I am no longer vicissitude's meek slave.

If a heart so full of love as mine can delight
without a temptation to torture me, I plead
for you to show me mercy in my plight.

But even if you have some perverse need
for cruelty and do not know wrong from right,
I am grateful to Love, the god whose commands I heed.

83

The hair at my temples has not yet turned white
(although time's salt and pepper have started to show),
but I still take precautions wherever I go,
lest I feel again Love's arrows' bite.

But if he should strike, it would not hurt me now
or not so much as back when I was young
and my heart was first pierced and my guts where wrung
while worry and despair wrinkled my brow.

No tears this time will well up in my eyes
although they know the way and the path they have made
running down my cheeks, and they could return.

But the fires are banked low. If a face should appear
to trouble my sleep a little, I am not afraid,
for there is no longer the fire by which I may burn.

84

"Weep, eyes, as you ought to do for your grave
transgression that has deeply wounded my heart."
"We do lament, but others played a part:
we were not the only ones to misbehave."

"It was through you that Love at first intruded
and through you he returns as if by right."
"We opened to him in hope of the delight
you sought. But we were both deluded."

"I suppose that you can claim I was complicit,
but it was through your greed that I was caught.
It was through you that Love made his first visit."

"What distresses us is that justice comes to naught
and we blame each other, which is not attractive, is it?
It's a lapse in the kind of behavior we were taught."

85

I have always been and shall remain a lover
ever more ardent with the passing days
even fond of the tears I shed and the ways
I suffer when Love assails me and takes over.

I cherish the day and hour when Love first came
to rid me of all my trivial concerns—
from a beautiful face like hers a lover learns
to pursue goodness for the sake of her sweet name.

It is not an easy path and is filled, God knows,
with obstacles and enemies on all sides.
But it does inspire one to virtuous deeds.

One fails, feels faint, but as long as hope abides
growing greater as desire grows,
one struggles onward, hearing that voice one heeds.

86

I have only contempt for that window from which
Love has shot his myriad arrows that may
wound but never kill—to die on a day
when life is nearly perfect is sweet and rich.

But languishing in the dungeon of this life
has brought me countless woes that hurt the more
because they abide with me. I am heart sore
and beyond the help of any surgeon's knife.

I've learned by now that no one can turn back
Time or rein it in as it rushes fast
and ruthless. I urge my soul under my breath:

"Go now! Your prospects are only shades of black
with all your best days irretrievably past
and a future of deterioration and death."

87

The instant the arrow flies from his taut bowstring,
the archer can tell which of his shots will go
astray; likewise his experienced fingers know
which will hit the bull's eye with its zing.

Just so, my Lady, you must have known right away
that the glance from your eyes had hit me deep and true
and that I was mortally hurt. You also knew
that the wound would weep forever from that day.

You said, with pity or mere curiosity, "What
will happen to him now? Where does this lead?
This was the fatal arrow that Love shot."

Now, however, that they have seen me bleed,
what my two enemies both desire is not
my death but a pain that makes me groan and plead.

88

From my hopes that were so long in coming true
and my life that I have wasted in this quest
I can see clearly now that it would have been best
to turn back, as a part of me always knew.

Now, I flee, but I am weak and lame
and deformed by years wasted in vanity.
The scars are on my face for the world to see
from the wars of Love for which I now feel shame.

So take my advice: "You who are tempted to go
on that sad way, turn back while you still can,
before you are burnt to a shell in Love's hot fires."

I have survived, a ruined and bitter man,
but none has escaped unhurt, for there was no
way to elude both her and his own desires

89

I fled the prison in which Love held me fast,
a slave to his caprice and cruel whim,
but having finally freed myself from him
I found my liberty bitter in contrast,

for my heart could not survive in the open air.
Along the way I met Love—in a disguise
that would, I think, have deceived sharper eyes
of a wiser man than I was then and there.

I confessed to him that I missed the shackles and chains
that now seemed even sweeter than going free.
He nodded in a sincere solicitude

as I told him of my error. Courteously
he explained to me that I had chosen my pains
myself—whom I could never hope to elude.

90

The breeze toyed with her golden tresses this
way and then that like a hairdresser trying one
look after another in creative fun,
and her eyes blazed with a brightness I now miss.

Her face showed color, in pity for me if not
affection. The tinder was dry within my heart.
It is not surprising then that this could start
a fire instantaneously hot.

Her gait was not a mortal's nor did her speech
sound like any earthly being's: she
appeared to be an angel who had descended.

But she was not the sun I took her to be,
as I would learn from what time had to teach.
The bow is slack now, but the pain has not ended.

91

That gentle Lady you loved so long and well
has left our midst and, I am sure, ascended
to the heaven toward which her every action tended
and where such creatures of special grace should dwell.

The time has come, then, to take back the keys
to your own heart that she held in her hand,
open the lock, and in a gesture grand
and glorious follow her in her decease.

Unburdened of your body's cumbrous weight
you will, like a pilgrim, rise higher and higher
gaining in knowledge as the view below

expands and clarifies until the entire
firmament presents itself, a great
and giddy vista only the angels know.

92

O ladies, weep, and let Love weep with you
through every land; O lovers weep, for he*
who gave his mind and soul entirely
to love is dead and honor is his due.

As for myself, I beg my grief to allow
tears to flow freely and sighs to break
for the comfort that they give and I may take
in mourning my dear friend who is absent now.

Let rhyme weep, too, for master Cino, who
explored the souls of men and showed us the way
to find the pain in beauty and beauty in pain.

And you, Pistoians, weep for him, all of you
having lost such an eminent man today,
but know that your grievous loss is heaven's gain.

---

* Cino da Pistoia (b. ca. 1265–1270, d. 1336), poet and Petrarch's friend.

93

How often has Love advised me, "Write what you've seen
in golden letters—how, among my powers,
I can change the colors of garden flowers
or make them grow or die as I intervene.

"You experienced this yourself not long ago
when you were a soloist in the lovers' chorus,
but you were wily and too determined for us,
and fled, but I caught you again, as you well know.

"If those lovely eyes of hers from which I first
revealed myself to you in order to soften
the hardness of your heart can do what they

"did and restore my broken bow, I may
cause you to weep bitterly and often
again with copious tears that will quench my thirst."

94

When that irresistible image comes into
my eyes and then my deepest heart to assume
absolute power, there is no more room
for the soul, which flees like a king the mob overthrew.

My limbs no longer take its orders but weigh
heavy and lifeless. But the exiled soul may find
a pleasant refuge somewhere, and the mind
can learn to take delight in its dismay.

Thus it can be that two faces both appear
pallid as if their deaths were imminent
their strength having disappeared in their content.

I witnessed this not long ago when I went
for a walk, and there were two lovers who, I fear,
resembled me, the lovesick sonneteer.

95

Could I express my thoughts in verse and suggest
the vividness they have within my heart,
no dolt in the world, encountering my art,
could fail to share the grief that is in my breast.

But I am stricken dumb by your blessed eyes
against whose blows I have no armor or shield.
You can see through me. My nature is revealed
in a nakedness no rhetoric can disguise.

Your vision is like a ray of the sun that can pass
through a window pane. Then let my passion speak
for itself better than I can ever do.

Neither Mary nor Peter had to seek
a confirmation of faith they knew to be true,
and for you my thoughts are all as transparent as glass.

96

I have waited so long that I begin to hate
the very thing I used to desire. Sighs
rasp in my throat and weeping has reddened my eyes.
I realize this, knowing it's far too late

and I cannot escape. Her image within me is bright
and I see it always and carry it everywhere.
It delights me while it drives me to a despair
from which I cannot escape, try as I might.

I went astray when my familiar road
was blocked to me as I tried to pursue a prize
simply for its beauty. One episode

and I was enthralled in a manner that defies
logic. My soul's allegiance now is owed
to one whom I adore but also despise.

97

O liberty, I see what your leaving meant
to my life, which was in an instant wholly changed:
the arrow struck me and I was at once deranged
in ways both fundamental and permanent.

My eyes cannot look away from the source of their woe,
no matter what my reason may say. They abhor
all other views and I cannot loiter before
a painting or pleasant building as I go.

I cannot listen to other talk than of death.
Her name resounds in my ears as the source of my
joy, and to it I devote all my breath.

My feet know no other path to take than toward
her. My hands are useless, too. I try
to write, but she is the subject of every word.

98

You can put reins on your charger and dictate
his movements, Orso,* but not your untamed heart,
which pursues honor and hates its counterpart,
disgrace, although meted out by a blind fate.

Do not sigh or be at all forlorn:
you are abed and must for a while absent
yourself from striving in any tournament.
You may reject all challenges with scorn.

Recover soon, and you will ride again
on the field in arms to show your birth and strength.
I know your heart will rejoice when that day arrives,

for you shall demonstrate clearly to all men
that although you have been absent, now at length
you have returned to the lists and shall survive.

------

* Orso dell' Anguillara, a friend of Petrarch.

99

Since you and I together have both found
how false our hopes have been, I think we should
lift up our hearts to seek a greater good
and search for happiness on higher ground.

This mortal life is a meadow where flowers bloom
on a grassy sward in which dread serpents lurk,
letting the beautiful scenery do its work
to lure us to it and to a wretched doom.

If you want a tranquil mind, then what you must do
is reject what most men desire and instead
try to emulate the wiser few

and change your life, for soon we are all dead.
Some will ask, with reason, "Who are you
to advise? Look where your own path has led!"

100

That window to the south from which the one
sun looks out at another up in the sky,
and the one on the north that winter breezes try
to rattle its frame until the cold is gone;

and that stone bench, which my Lady sits upon
alone, thoughtful, her fingers interlaced;
and all the places her lovely form has graced
and floors her feet have sometimes trodden on;

that lofty fastness where I was first waylaid
by Love; and that first day of spring when all
my ancient wounds reopen and bleed on cue;

and most of all that face that I recall
in brightest day and nighttime's deepest shade—
these cause my tears to well up fresh and new.

101

Implacable she pardons none who live
in the world. Time yields us and then forgets
our lives and names. These are burdensome debts
on which Death gives no extensions and never forgives.

All this yearning, and yet, within my heart
I can feel the rumble of thunder from the last
day. But even so, Love holds me fast
so that my breath will catch and tears will start.

Seconds and minutes nibble our years away
and I understand this and am not deceived
but am subject to a power stronger than I.

My passion and reason are engaged in an unrelieved
struggle of many years, which the latter may
win if down here we can know what they know on high.

102

When Egypt's traitor handed Caesar the head
of Pompey, it is said he wept at this,
concealing the boundless joy that must have been his
beholding the grisly proof that his foe was dead.

And Hannibal, when he saw how the fates had turned
against him and the Carthaginians, laughed
even as they all wept. He was not daft,
but to show his hurt was a weakness that he spurned.

So it can happen that men will find ways to hide
feelings with a show of their opposites
with their faces not announcing what is inside.

And often if I am laughing or singing, it's
perversity on my part or mere pride
that I can still assert with my addled wits.

103*

Hannibal, victorious, did not know
how to exploit his success. Be careful, then,
that you do not turn out to be one of those unlucky men
who see their triumphs melt away like snow.

The she-bear,[†] furious at the loss of her poor
cubs, will burn with rage and sharpen her claws
to execute one of nature's harshest laws
and take the bloody revenge she is waiting for.

So, when she is riled again, keep your sword's blade
sharp and be prepared to defend your name
and life if one of your enemies appears.

Do not seek out a fight; behave the same
as you always do, but do not be afraid,
and your fame and honor will last for a thousand years.

---

* Stefano Colonna defended himself against two members of the Orsini
family by killing them.
† Orsini, in Italian, means bearish.

104

That excellent virtue in you* that blossomed forth
when you and Love first grappled produces fruit
worthy of those flowers, while my pursuit
of happiness benefits from your great worth.

I feel impelled to write your praises here
in verse, which is more than any sculptor can do.
No piece of marble can move or speak like you
in life, which is how your lordship deserves to appear.

Do Caesar's bust or Marcellus's smile or speak?
Do Paulus or Africanus ever blink?
Whatever the hammer, chisel, and anvil may seek,

what they produce is inert. Pandolfo, I think
if marble can shatter to a few antique
fragments, we're better off with pen and ink.

---

* Pandolfo Malatesta, ruler of Rimini.

106*

On nimble wings, a little angel came down
from Heaven to appear on the springtime strand
where Fortune had directed my feet one day

and, having observed that I was quite alone,
she spread her diaphanous net upon the sand
where the gentle breezes make beach grass sway.

She caught me, which is not a great surprise,
but I cannot complain in the gaze of her lovely eyes.

---

* A madrigal.

107

I see neither escape nor hope of relief,
for her eyes have so long been assailing me
with torment that only my mortality
can promise an end to my heart's constant grief.

I would flee, but where can I hide from the bright beams
of her dazzling eyes? It's fifteen years now and I
am as stunned as I was at the start, or more, and on my
brain her image is graven, awake and in dreams.

There is nowhere I can hide from the brilliant light
that flashes on all sides so her face is there
radiant. As in tales that children read,

one sprig of laurel has turned to a thicket where
I am led astray and cannot find the right
path. I follow wherever Love may lead.

108

O fortunate dirt, where Love once set her shoe!
She was, as it happens, coming in my direction,
and the breezes hushed in a show of respect and affection
as natural phenomena seldom do.

Were her figure carved in adamant life-sized,
it would wear smooth before I could forget
her passing here. It is vivid to me yet
in a memory I have most highly prized.

However often our paths may intersect,
I look down at the earth where your light tread
has left its touch and treasure it. Don't laugh,

and don't believe me, but go to ask, instead,
my friend Sennuccio* if I am not correct.
He'll offer you a sigh on my behalf.

---

* Sennuccio del Bene, a friend of Petrarch and a Florentine poet.

109

Again and again, thousands of times, Love has
assaulted me ferociously day and night,
but I return to where I first saw the light
of the sparks that blazed up in my heart and was

therefore a sacred spot. It still repairs—
at nones and vespers, matins and angelus—
my soul to a peace and calm that are glorious
such that I forget all my other cares.

A gentle breeze comes from her serene
face, and the sounds of her carefully measured words
sweeten the azure sky and gentle the air.

The place is a perfectly paradisiacal scene
that comforts me with the liturgy of the birds
I hear, and I breathe freely only there.

110

Like a man who has armed himself and is ready to fight
in a battle, I refortified all my defenses
and waited for Love once more to assault my senses,
prepared with what I had learned and knew was right.

Close by I saw a shadow darken the earth
blocking out the sunlight, and its shady
shape I recognized as that of my Lady
whom I have praised and revered for her heavenly worth.

I asked myself why I should feel fear
but even before that thought was formed, the rays
of sudden warmth that came from being near

my Lady seized me to enrapture and amaze.
It was like a close bolt of lightning when you hear
the thunderclap while the sky is still ablaze.

111

The lady whose face is graven in my heart
passed by where I was sitting, thinking of her,
and there she was in fact, as if she were
conjured up from my brooding. It gave me a start

but I rose and bowed, and she saw how my face was wan
and drawn, and she deigned to smile at me with a sweet
expression that could, I have no doubt, defeat
Jove's rage, which in an instant would be gone.

I tried to speak before she walked away
but I could not bear the gentleness of her look
nor endure the brilliance of her lovely gaze,

but such was the deep pleasure my soul took
that when I think of her greeting on that day
no grief can touch me, whatever Fate essays.

112

Sennuccio,* I write to let you know
that I'm still the same, no better if no worse;
I burn, I melt. I need not here rehearse
my inconstancies: I go where the breezes blow

and feel what she makes me feel. She is haughty or kind,
is cruel, is full of mercy, is glum, is gay,
and to all these moods of hers, I react or, say,
overreact, and I think I am losing my mind.

She sat over there and sang. Or here, she turned
and smiled. Or in that corner she stopped and stood
and she glanced in my direction, and I was stricken

so that I blushed and felt that my face burned.
Over there she furrowed her brow, which boded no good.
Love afflicts me, and day by day I sicken.

---

* Sennuccio del Bene, Petrarch's friend. See 108.

113

Sennuccio mio, I come here only half
a man, wishing that I were whole and you,
at peace. The winds are howling as they do
when the gods are angry and either rage or laugh.

But I have no dread of storms and stare at the sky
defying the lightning and the thunder's roll
because I am serene deep in my soul,
and I shall be delighted to tell you why.

I believe in the land of lovers where the breeze
is gentle, calming the air and the cloudburst's roar
so that the wildest elements turn meek.

Love and my Lady rule my soul, and these
have rekindled the fire so that I fear no more,
for her gaze makes all the mighty powers weak.

114

From impious Babylon* from which all sense
of shame has fled and every virtue as well,
the mother of all error, another hell,
I, too, have decamped, proceeding thence

to a quieter, happier life here in the Vaucluse,†
where I pass the pleasant and uninterrupted hours
gathering sometimes rhymes and sometimes flowers,
an existence few men can imagine, let alone choose.

I do not worry much about Fortune or fame,
or even about myself. Such vulgar concerns
cannot engage me in this delightful place.

My worries are only two: I need not name
her, the woman for whom my spirit burns,
and him whose foot I trust will heal apace.‡

---

* The papal court at Avignon.
† The "closed valley" from which the River Sorgue arises, not far from Avignon.
‡ Probably Giovanni Colonna.

115

I knew a lady, chaste and proud, who stood
between two lovers, one a lord who rules
men, holds power, and is decked in silks and jewels,
the other, me, trying as hard as I could.

He looked away, which she took as disregard,
and then she turned, perhaps in pride, to me,
with a pleasant mien I had never expected to see
but which I rejoiced to have as Fate's reward.

My jealousy changed now into delight
and I could hardly breathe for happiness,
seeing that my impressive rival was gone.

And he? A moment of unpleasantness
and a brief scowl of puzzlement that he might
be bested in a contest he'd thought he'd won.

116

Filled with that ineffable sweetness my eyes
draw forth now from her beautiful face, I find
that I need nothing else; my heart and mind
have agreed to reject and even to despise

all other, lesser beauty. I bid good-bye
to the life I trained for. Whatever isn't she
is otiose and irrelevant to me,
uninteresting and unable to satisfy.

In a closed-in valley* I find an anodyne
for my pains and sighs. Pensive, here, and slow,
I am alone with Love, which is all I want.

No ladies are here, and yet, wherever I go
among the stones and springs, there is the benign
memory, soothing, and faithfully revenant.

---

* In Italian, *valle chiusa,* in French, *Vaucluse,* which is its name.

117

If the wall of the Vaucluse were to rearrange
itself so that, out of fastidiousness,
it turned its back on Babylon's shamelessness
to face toward Rome, it would be a welcome change,

for my hopes and sighs would have an easier road.
Now they wander scattered and make their way
however they can toward Rome, where I hope they
arrive safely, bearing up under their load.

There they are received and welcomed with such
friendly warmth that they remain and do not
return, for there they thrive where they like to be.

I wish them well, but every day I have got
to hold back my sobs and tears that very much
want to join in their felicity.

118

Sixteen years of torment have come and gone,
and I am getting older prematurely,
but the start of my pain is still so vivid that, surely,
its onset could have been yesterday afternoon.

I've developed a taste for bitterness and woe
and have learned to put them to use, but still my load
is heavy and I fear that my life's road
will come to an end before I am ready to go.

Here I am, though I wish to be elsewhere
and dare not even dream of any more.
I do the best I can and muddle through.

My new tears reassure me some, for they're
proof that I haven't changed. What I was before,
I remain still and have been faithful to.

120

For your fine canzone* about my death that displays
such grace and talent, I take up my pen
first of all to thank you sincerely, but then
to reassure you that I'm alive (the phrase

is "still on the green side of the grass,") although
the door we all face and dread cannot
be far away. I had approached it but
discovered that I did not yet have to go.

On the door's lintel I saw that the time ordained
for me had not quite ended and I turned
back, to enjoy what little of it remained.

I could not read the inscription and have not learned
the day of my death. But I send my unfeigned
thanks for your poem and your having been concerned.

---

* Antonio de Ferrara, having heard a rumor of Petrarch's death, wrote a poem
of mourning for him.

121[*]

Look, Love, at the young lady—despite
your rule and my pains, she doesn't care at all.
Between two adversaries of no small

puissance, she stands alone, secure and quite
unafraid. You're armored; she's in a gown
and, barefoot among the flowers, sits herself down

and is cruel to me while she gives you a haughty frown.
I am her helpless captive, but you could take
revenge with a single arrow for pity's sake.

---

[*] A madrigal.

122

Seventeen years have passed since the fire first
burned me, and now whenever I contemplate
my plight I find, in my pitiable state,
a chill as well. And I cannot quench my thirst.

The adage says that one's hair will change before
one's habits do. Of course, I am growing old
and the fever in the blood is turning cold
in my carapace: I know what is in store.

When will that day come when my soul shall rise
like an ember from a fire into the air
to bring at last an end to my trials down here?

I like to imagine the scene I'll encounter there:
her face smiling in welcome before my eyes
in a perfect and harmonious atmosphere.

123

Her face was pale but it glowed as if there were
a cloud through which the sun of her smile shone.
and my heart, in a joy that it had never known,
came forth to meet it and to delight in her.

I knew then how in Paradise one can see
and comprehend another, soul to soul,
and I felt a heavenly rapture as my whole
being joined hers in a perfect congruity.

Her kindly looks or humble gestures seemed
insulting or derisive when compared
to that perfect union in which I knew her heart,

and then, as if in a scene that I had dreamed,
she gazed into my eyes and as I stared
back, asked, "Who has been keeping us apart?"

124

Love, Fortune, and my own troubled mind
that closes its eyes to the present, future, and past
afflict me so that, helplessly downcast,
I envy those who have left their lives behind.

Love plagues my heart; Fortune takes away
the comforts I have enjoyed; and my mind pines
in constant low-grade anguish that undermines
my soul: I have forgotten how to pray.

I do not expect good times again or that what
I wanted will come true. A slow decline
with diminutions now but no increases.

My hopes slip from my hand, not diamonds but
mere cut glass, and every dream of mine
shatters on the floor in a thousand pieces.

130

Finding that Mercy's road was barred to me,
I took another desperate track as far
away as I could be from those eyes that are
the beginning and end of my fidelity.

I feed my heart with sighs and live on tears,
which satisfy my tastes. I do not complain:
it seems I was born for weeping and for pain,
which can be sweeter than it first appears.

A single image blazes in my mind,
not by a Phidias or Praxitiles
but by an artist of a higher kind.

What distant spot in the antipodes
can hide me so that Envy cannot find
me out with its relentless energies?

131

I would sing of Love but in a new
way that would convert her tears and sighs
to celebrations that take her by surprise,
warm her gelid heart, and even bedew

her cheeks with compassionate tears as her regret
blossoms within her for all the pain that she
has caused, however inadvertently,
but now admits and wishes to forget.

I'd perform magic to makes red roses bloom
in white snowdrifts and discover ivory
that transforms into marble all who look

upon it. I can learn to bear this gloom
in my brief time on earth, if this must be
the way I get into fame's exclusive book.

132

If it is not Love, then what do I feel?
Or, if it is, then what kind can it be?
How can it be good if it's bitter to me?
Or, it's bad, how can it have such appeal?

If I want this, then why do I lament?
If I don't, then what is the use of protesting so?
It's a living death! A delicious kind of woe!
How can it rule me without my consent?

If I do consent, why do I still complain?
I am at sea, tossed as the winds contend,
in a rudderless boat, with neither compass nor chart.

I don't know these waters or even the course I intend
to follow. I observe as my own brain
issues absurd commands to my mutinous heart.

133

Love uses me as a target as the sun
delights in melting snow or the hot fire
enjoys the melting of wax, or, going higher,
the wind likes driving clouds along for fun.

The fatal shot came at me from your eyes,
and there was nowhere I could hide or take
shelter from that weapon by which you make
the sun and wind and fire your allies.

Thoughts are your arrows, and your face is the bright
sun, while passion is your fire, and these
dazzle me and reduce me to helplessness.

Your song, your speech in which I take delight
overwhelm all my feeble energies
while before your gentle breezes* I deliquesce.

---

* Petrarch has a pun here on Laura and *l'aura* (breeze) that is impossible to render in English.

134

There is no peace and I am unarmed for war;
I hope and fear, I freeze and yet I burn;
I look about and everywhere I turn
are paradoxes I am not ready for.

I am not locked up and yet I am not free.
She will not keep me but will not send me away.
I am not killed but tormented day by day:
Love cannot decide which is worse for me.

I have no eyes but I see. I have no tongue
and yet I speak. I want to die but call
for help. I hate myself but love her still.

I feed on pain, mix peals of laughter among
my sobs, and I am full of hatred for all
creation. And this is at my Lady's will.

136

Let flame from the skies rain down upon your hair,
malevolent ones, who delight in wickedness.
You found that acorns and water are rather less
tasty than that elaborate, richer fare

you blithely extort from the poor. The ills of the world—
intemperance, gluttony, sloth, and greed—that the Fall
brought us are now your pleasures and habits, and all
the flags of Beelzebub's minions are unfurled.

Old men chase nubile girls around in your
palaces while the servants look away,
pretending an interest in the grotesque décor.

You, who were not reared sumptuously, may
try to forget your youth, but what is in store
in your future is hell's own stench on judgment day.

137

In its greed, Babylon has stuffed its sack
with the burden of God's righteous anger, promoting
Venus and Bacchus rather than devoting
itself to Jove and Athena. I cry, Alack!

and wait for a cruel justice, perhaps in the form
of Moors from Baghdad, who may come to hold
court and seize their captives to be sold
as slaves in a place where such excess is the norm.

Her idols will be smashed and scattered on
the earth; her towers will be consumed in fire
with all their keepers in them. When they are gone,

the lovely righteous souls we all admire
will rule again, and this will be the dawn
of the golden age to which we should aspire.

138

Fountain of sorrows, dwelling place of ire,
school of error, and temple of heresy,
arrived from Rome to France only to be
another Babylon, where the good expire

and the wicked thrive in confusion's dismal den,
a hell for the living where minor devils play
as if they had no fear of the judgment day
when Christ shall punish all such sinful men!

You once were chaste and humble but now are
rebels and shameless whores who have lost all hope
of redemption. You are thieves who rob the poor.

Constantine, who gave popes power, is far
below in the hell with which you will have to cope,
sharing his exquisite tortures evermore.

139

The more I flutter my wings to join you all
in Italy, the tighter my fate's hold
that keeps me here with obstacles untold
and frustrates my response to your friendship's call.

In dreams I see the Venetian landscapes below
the mountains that the sky seems to embrace,
where my happy heart sojourns in its chosen place
and to which, if I could manage it, I'd go.

My heart and I diverged when I went west
and he kept going straight, so I am here
in Egypt while his path, by far the best,

took him to Jerusalem. I find cheer
in supposing that we will both be blessed
and reunited. I hope that day is near.

140

Love, who rules my life, has made his seat
of power in my heart, but there are times
when ambition strikes him and he arms and climbs
up to my head to triumph in my defeat.

But she, to whom we are both devoted, reproves
both him and me, for reason ought to reign
with shame and reverence in any gentleman's brain
and order his emotions and how he loves.

Love then decamps and retreats, undone, afraid
that what he has dared will ruin both of us
and he cowers in my heart. The mistake he's made

will bring disaster. I come to his aid
and comfort him: his venture was valorous
and I do not condemn the action he essayed.

141

Sometimes in summer, there comes a butterfly
that flutters at random but then, drawn by the light,
follows its desire and aims its flight
at the glitter of a lovely human eye

where it dies and also causes pain. And I
am like the lepidopteran that in season
abandons whatever prudence it has and reason
to annoy what it has been enraptured by.

They leave me alone, recognizing that we
have much in common, for I don't mind the pain
I feel, but am tormented when I see

discomfort in another. If I am slain
my soul is resigned, pleased that she will be
rid of a nuisance and not bothered again.

143

Hearing your sweet discourse, I think that Love
himself were instructing all his pupils and my
dormant passions flame, rekindled by
words even a corpse would take notice of.

I remember my sweet Lady and those rare
times she was kind to me. Now I awake
not to bright bells but to sobs and sighs that break
my heart from which they arise into the air.

I see her turn and the breeze caresses her
hair, so that, wherever else she goes,
she strolls into my heart, which is her own.

But I lack the words to say how this can stir
my soul and lift my spirits or disclose
how she rules me as if from a royal throne.

144

There are spectacular sunrises some days
when the sky is cloudless and a delicate blue,
or, after showers, a rainbow can happen that you
can't quite believe with colors that amaze.

On such a day, I first saw that special face
transform itself in a blaze of light to find
a resonance in my eyes and heart and mind
that put me—dare I say?—in a state of grace.

I looked on Love, who turned her eyes to me
and from that time until this moment all
else in the world appears to be dark and dead.

Sennuccio, since his arrow struck me, he
has ruled my life: I am at his beck and call,
and only he—and she—are in my head.

145

Put me where the sun scorches the earth
or where he is bested by constant ice and snow
or put me in territory where he can go
in moderation, in plenitude or dearth;

give me good fortune or a run of terrible luck,
put me in pleasant air or miasmic fens,
make it daytime or night that never ends,
make me old or make me a gay young buck;

put me in Heaven, or earth, or in the abyss,
on a mountain peak or in a deep valley, assign
mobility to me or deny me this

and keep me always in one place that's mine:
I'll be what I have always been, which is
a master of sighs that I perfect and refine.

146

Oh, splendid soul, temple of virtue, for you
I fill page after page with absolute
devotion, chaste fortress whom no pursuit
by men can threaten or bring annoyance to,

oh, flame, oh, roses blossoming in the snow,
a mirror in whom I see what I should be,
and bringing whose pleasure is always a joy to me,
so that I extend my wings and try to show

how much you grace the world. If rhymes could spread
and still make sense, I'd let the Greenlanders hear
how fine you are and the Bedouins in the sand.

But among those people, my language is, I fear,
opaque so I shall sing your praise instead
in Italy where perhaps they will understand.

147

My ardent desire sometimes rides me hard
with sharp spurs and a cruel bit, hell-bent
for leather, turning wild and violent,
surprising me, and catching me off guard.

He finds one who can understand my will
and also see the fear within my heart,
and then he sees those flashes of anger that start
from my Lady's eyes and chasten with their chill.

Thereupon he flees as one in a storm
upon whom thunderbolts crack down from heaven
as fear routs my desire instantly.

Then, having averted serious harm,
the images of her face return that are graven
in my heart to reprove and comfort me.

148

Not the Tiber, the Arno, or the Po,
or, for that matter, the Indus, Tigris, or Nile,
the Danube, the Don, the Rhine, the Rhone, or, while
I'm listing rivers, the Alph, or the Ebro's flow

can quench the fire in my sad heart. The Loire?
The famous Hebrus in Greece? Or France's Seine?
None of them, or my friend, the Sorgue, my main
comfort here in the Vaucluse . . . Rivers are

cold comfort for Love's distress. I have a tree,
a laurel I planted here on the bank. Its shade
is where I sit and write. It pleases me

and settles my mind so that I am not afraid
to essay performances in poetry,
on guard against Love who will, again, invade.

149*

From time to time her cold beauty seems
to warm me and she gives me a sweet smile
as if in one of my dreams
and in her eyes a kindly aspect gleams.

My sighs are confused that long expressed my pain
and soothed my anguished heart.
I had mastered the art
of imposing a pleasing finish upon my sadness.
But how can I continue to complain
when I look at her and start
to wonder if Love's dart
has not stricken her, too, and brought his madness?
Still, can I hope for anything but badness
when a moment of peace is likely to be a deceit
so my ruin will be complete
with my hopes raised and dashed by Love's cruel schemes.

---

* A ballata

150

—What do you think, old Soul. Will we have peace?
A brief truce? Or war that keeps on going?—
—About the future, there is no way of knowing.
But her gentle eyes have hints of a surcease.—

—But her eyes can be ice in summertime or fire
in the dead of winter. They are not easy to read.—
—It's Love you should ask or, rather, to whom you should
    plead.—
—Then it's difficult for us to judge her desire.—

—Sometimes she does not speak but in her heart
cries out in pain, although her face is gay,
and she's weeping where your eyes cannot discern.—

—My mind is yet unsatisfied. She would betray
such inner turmoil, however great her art,
as wretchedness, my master, has made me learn.—

151

No weary helmsman ever made it to port
escaping the raging winds and whipping spume
with more relief than I feel, fleeing the gloom
to which my passion drives me for its sport;

no holy light has dazzled human eyes
more completely than I have been stunned by hers
with their fatally beautiful rays that Love prefers
when he takes aim with his bow to dispatch his prize.

He is not blind: I see him draw the string.
He is naked except for a gesture of modesty,
the boy with wings that painters have portrayed.

But what he hides from others he shows to me
within her lovely eyes of which I sing
of Love that makes me proud but also afraid.

152

So meek, but fierce and wild, with a tiger's heart
but a human face and she can even appear
in an angel's form: torn between hope and fear
I spin faster and faster and fly apart.

My life is over unless she welcomes me
or lets me go—either one will do.
Meanwhile I despair between these two,
reduced to an utter immobility.

My spirit cannot bear this vacillation
between burning and freezing, red as fire
or blue as the coldest glacier in creation.

It has learned that its only hope is to expire
and it languishes and loses animation
in dreams of the cold ground or a funeral pyre.

153

Go, you hot sighs, to melt her heart's hard ice
and with your burning turn her frigidity
to a tolerable temperature for me
as prayers bring mercy to sinners from paradise.

Go forth, sweet thoughts, to speak to her and show
the wonders of the earth that she cannot see,
and if she remains aloof and cruel to me
our hopes will die and our torments also.

Both sighs and thoughts can tell, or at least imply,
how grave our present plight is and appeal
to her, for only she can mollify

our torment. Address her heart, which is not steel,
and Love will go with you and will stand close by
to bear his witness to the pain you feel.

154

The stars of heaven and all the elements
combine to make the living light we see
where Nature and the sun so radiantly
rule and impose on inert matter sense.

It is an awesome and staggering display
we cannot look at directly or even think
too long about, for mind and eyes will blink
while Love's sweetness rains down every day.

The air is as clear and pure as chastity,
beyond our thoughts or words of gratitude
in a place from which all base desires flee,

and the firmament is thoroughly imbued
with honor. In this world there cannot be
threats to great beauty from the base or lewd.

155

Neither Caesar nor mighty Jove were so stern
as not to be moved by pity and put by
their usual weapons, hearkening to the cry
of those from whose pains they could not turn:

Love brought me to my Lady to hear her groans
of lamentation that filled my heart with woe
and desire as well. To know that she suffered so
struck me to the marrow of my bones.

What he had shown me, he transmogrified
into art, the words of which he wrote
with a diamond pen upon my heart to abide

forever. In random moments however remote,
should I need reminding, he can find inside
my heart those sighs that issued from her throat.

156

I have seen aspects of angels here on earth
and encountered beauties from far beyond our sphere:
everything else that is visible down here
is smoke and shadow of neither weight nor worth.

I have seen those lovely lights when they
were weeping that make the sun feel envious
and have heard sighs and sobs so dolorous
as to stop rivers or move mountains away.

Sorrow, piety, love, and wisdom combined
to make a sweeter music than my ear
has ever heard before or than my mind

has ever imagined. Nature, the better to hear,
froze so that no leaf stirred in a silence designed
to let that sweetness pervade the atmosphere.

157

A bitter day but honored nonetheless
that I can never forget—the image will
be fixed in my heart and in my mind until
all thought and feeling dwindle to nothingness.

Her gracious gestures, her piteous laments
made me wonder what kind of creature she
was—a mortal or might she more likely be
a goddess, who filled the sky with radiance?

Hair gold, face snow, her arched delicate brows
were ebony, and her bright eyes shone starlight.
Near her, Love's arrows never missed their mark.

Each word she spoke was like a perfect rose,
but sorrowful to make the world contrite.
And her tears gleamed like crystals in the dark.

158

No matter where I turn my eyes for relief,
I find that my imagination has placed
my Lady's portrait, and every wall is graced
with her image to renew my wounds of grief.

Worse, the image speaks sweet words to express
her deep compassion and even her regret
for my torment and, though I am grateful, yet
I suffer for her kindnesses' duress.

Love and truth were with me when I said
how her beauty was unmatched anywhere
in the world, nor have I ever heard or read

of anyone so kindly or so fair
as that gleam upon her cheeks from tears she has shed,
like diamonds but more valuable and rare.

159

From what Platonic heaven could have come
the Idea from which Nature built that face,
that perfect physiognomy to trace
and impose on matter, malleable and dumb?

What nymph lounging beside a babbling stream
or dryad in the woods could ever comb
such golden hair? What heart was ever home
to so many signal virtues that I esteem?

For those who believe that beauty is divine,
the search ends here, when they at last behold
her eyes and see how lively is their shine.

Such perfection as I have here extolled
carries danger: I feel my spirits decline
that her laughter can revive a hundredfold.

160

Neither Love nor I are able to gauge
someone like her, whose words or laughter can
melt the heart of any god or man.
In our book her name stands alone on the page.

Her eyes shine out beneath a brow of pure
serenity, and they guide me with their light.
For no other beacons, either to left or right,
do I adjust my course of which I am sure.

On the grass, she can blossom like a flower
or, hugging a tree, she can make it bloom
in any season as some wood nymph might.

To watch her walk alone in a verdant bower
lost in her brooding's elegant perfume
is to be transformed forever by the sight.

161

Oh, staggering steps, oh, longing fantasies,
oh, memories and ardor intertwined,
oh, constant passion, troubling my mind,
oh, eyes, who weep from constant miseries—

oh, laurel leaves that honor famous brows,
oh, life so full of contrarieties
where error is sweet and ambiguities
send me to search for more than heaven allows;

oh, lovely face where Love equipped with both
spurs and reins with which he goads me on
and checks me, while I cannot throw him down;

oh, noble amorous souls whom I am loath
to trouble, and you poor souls who are dead and gone,
the suffering you have known is also my own!

162

How happy are the flowers and fortunate grass
on which my Lady sometimes strolls in thought,
and the beach sand which from time to time has caught
a word or may hope for a footprint were she to pass.

I envy the slender trees with leafy boughs
that dapple the sunshine on violets below
in the shady woods where sometimes she may go
delicately as if in a dream or drowse.

O, gentle countryside where the river runs
at which she glances with her approving eyes
that in their turn illuminate like suns

I'd long for your chaste good fortune but I surmise
the tiniest pebble among you that she stuns
burns with the passion I feel and demonize.

163

Love, who can see clearly into my mind
as well as ahead where you guide my treacherous steps,
consider what is hidden away in my depths
and give me your honest judgment of what you find.

You know how I have suffered, for you know
how arduous is the path you set for me.
I am weak to exhaustion but do not see
mercy or any relenting as I go.

In the far distance, I see that radiant light
toward which you drive me mercilessly, but I
do not have your wings by which I might

make better progress. And yet you satisfy
my wildest passions, giving me not flight
but ardor. And she is pleased to hear me sigh.

164

In the heavens the winds have fallen silent, and sleep
has hushed the wild beasts and the birds. In the sky
the silent constellations are wheeling by,
and the drowse of the waveless sea in its bed is deep.

Only I am awake, thinking in sweet
ruinous pain of her who is always there
before my eyes. In the dark she is everywhere
and my only consolation in defeat.

Thus from the one fountain comes the bad
and the good in my life. From one hand can come
the wound as well as its cure or its anodyne.

My suffering is endless and drives me mad
with a thousand hurts that never seem to numb.
I do not die, but health is not yet mine.

165

Across the grass her white foot all but floats
and from each footstep radiates a power
to enrich each blade and invigorate each flower
her careless passage graces and promotes.

Love pays attention only to noble hearts
ignoring his collateral effects,
but as light diffuses, refracts, and reflects
so does her great power and his arts.

Her gentle glance, her words, her graceful gait
and her measured gestures carried me away,
although she was always decorous and sedate.

From small sparks come great fires, as you may
see in my passions she could not anticipate.
I am a helpless night bird at midday.

166

If I had remained in that cave where Apollo once
became a prophet, Florence perhaps could claim,
as Verona, Mantua, and Arunca, the same
distinction of having a poet among her sons.*

From my fields no green rushes ever come,
lacking the proper moisture. I must toil
mowing thorns and thistles from meager soil,
with a crooked scythe that I grow weary from.

Even Athena's olive tree is dry,
Parnassus's freshets trickling down elsewhere
so that the parched ground shows here and there.

In just such fashion will my poor talent fare,
unless great Jove, moved to compassion by
my plight, sends rain, without which I will die.

---

* Dante would not have counted because he wrote in Italian. Verona,
  Mantua, and Arunca were the birthplaces of Catullus, Virgil, and Juvenal.

167

It's Love that makes her lower her lovely eyes
and who uses his hands to sculpt her breath into
a sigh that comes from somewhere in the blue
heavens, and during all this I realize

that my heart is being stolen out of my chest.
My thoughts are different and what I am wishing for.
Heaven has made this martyrdom for a poor
acolyte, who is cursed but also blessed.

My soul is ready to depart but my senses,
drunk with sweetness, pull me back from the lip
of death's abyss for at least a little while.

For what is fated, there are no defenses:
the siren* winds the spool that measures my trip
here on earth while the three Fates smile.

---

* Er, who governs a heavenly sphere and whose music maintains the harmony
  of the world.

168

Love sends me a delicious thought that is
the go-between for the two of us to say
that I am making progress on my way
toward what I have yearned for, that perfect bliss.

His speech is sometimes true and sometimes not.
I cannot trust him and don't know how to take
his words—well-wishing? Lies? Or a mere mistake?
Or something else? But I cannot imagine what.

The days meanwhile go by and as they do
my hopes and confidence fade and my doubts grow
as relentless age nags me with minor pains.

But everyone gets old: that's nothing new.
My desire declares a rousing "No!"
but still I wonder how much time remains.

169

One fixed idea, one longing separates me
from other men so I am all alone
and would even hide from myself in some unknown
fastness from this obsessive fantasy.

But then she walks by, cruel and yet so sweet
that my soul flutters its wings and in vain tries
to fly. She is guarded by an army of sighs
and is confident of Love's and my own defeat.

If I am not mistaken, I see a gleam
of pity in her eyes, which soothes my heart
at least a little. Or did I imagine it?

I gather up my soul and my self-esteem
and prepare to describe my wretched plight in art,
but with so much to say, I lack the words and wit.

170

How many times have I taken courage from
the reports of my eyes about her gentle smile
so that I had the nerve at least for a while
to address her, confident that the words would come.

But then her expression changes and my brave
moment passes. It is my destiny
and the tragedy of my life that I should be
entirely in her power, her pawn, her slave.

The result is that I never can say a word
that anyone but me can understand
because Love urges me on and then lets me fall.

Desire can tie one's tongue and turn one's grand
utterances to foolishness. It's absurd.
One who can say he's in love isn't at all.

171

Love has put me in the grasp of fair
but cruel arms, and if I make complaint
they squeeze me more tightly so that I all but faint.
Better to keep still with this pain I bear,

for she could dry the Rhine with her angry eyes
or melt its ice in winter. She is so proud
that my being pleased with her beauty isn't allowed
and her disdain she does not try to disguise.

Her heart is as hard as diamond and I cannot make
any slightest scratch upon its shine,
while the rest of her is marble that can move.

But her black looks at me can never take
away the stubborn hopes that remain mine,
or the sighs and tears that arise out of my love.

172

Oh, Envy, you old foe of virtue, you
are opposed even to first steps toward the good.
What hidden pathway did you take that could
have brought you into that lovely breast to do

worse than your usual damage? You've ruined me,
letting her think that I was a fortunate lover.
She thought I was chaste and humble, but to discover
the opposite angered her, irretrievably.

She weeps about what she thinks is my success
with other women and laughs at my own tears,
but she cannot change my heart that nevertheless

loves her. Over and over again it hears
her insults, but I shall continue to address
her with fervor, despite my nagging fears.

173

I admire the clear sun of her lovely eyes,
even while Love makes mine bloodshot and wet;
my wretched soul endeavors to forget
me and find a place in paradise,

but for its sweet dream, there is bitter waking
to a failure it must accept. The world is dust
and spiderwebs, and my soul then makes a just
complaint to Love for causing it such aching.

It writhes between extremes: its reception is cold
and its longing burning, and it therefore is in part
happy but also full of misery.

Its sanguine thoughts are few, but a thousandfold
are gloomy ones of its injuries that smart.
Such is the fruit that comes from this rare tree.

174

Cruel star (that has, as we suppose,
powers for good or bad) underneath whom
I was bred and born into the gloom
of a hard life in a world of bruises and blows,

and you, cruel Lady, whose eyes Love likes to use
as weapons of warfare with which to inflict
deep wounds upon a victim he has picked,
it is within your power, if you should choose,

to use them as cures, for your heart is not so hard
as that of Love. Your glances are not spears
but only little arrows that do not kill,

and that gives me much comfort, for I regard
longing for her who has no earthly peers
as better than loving another—and always will.

175

When I think back upon the time and place
where I first lost myself in Love's tight knot,
which he fastened with his own hands, making what
was bitter sweet and tears a mark of grace,

I am tinder and sulfur, and my heart
burns with a bright fire that rages there
to light my life so that I do not care
for the rest of the world but only this tiny part.

The sun that shines only for me all day
continues to warm me, even when night comes on,
as much as she did at noon when the weather was hot.

She gives me sustenance even from far away,
for that memory I treasure is never gone
of the time, the place, and the tight beloved knot.

176

The woods are hostile and wild, but in their dense
midst where even armed men feel some fear,
I travel safe and secure, confident here
except for the sun against which there's no defense,

for its rays are like Love that prompts me to my song
of her who is always present, accompanied by
her maids and other ladies—which is how I
figure the beeches and firs I pass among.

It is her voice I hear in the sough overhead
of the wind in the branches, the songs of the darting birds,
and the babble of the brook in its winding run.

Seldom have the woods, so full of dread,
offered instead such pleasure beyond all words—
except the worry that I may lose my sun.

177

In a single day, Love has been my guide
to a thousand rivers; a thousand mountains appear,
for wingèd shoes are a part of his followers' gear,
and they soar in the third sphere in a splendid ride.

It is fine to be deep in the Ardennes
unarmed, where Mars lurks hidden in the trees.
My ship has neither mast nor rudder: on seas
of thought it drifts, catches, and drifts again.

But the light is waning now as my courage does,
and I think how I arrived here and am amazed.
I want to return home that always was

my comfortable place where cattle grazed
beside my familiar river and that also has
been the spot on which my sun has blazed.

178

Love spurs me on but also holds me back,
comforts and terrifies me, burns and freezes,
is kind, is cruel, behaves however he pleases,
lights up my life with hope and then goes black.

He raises me up only to dash me down,
and wearies my heart as it wanders hither and yon
so that it hates what it has been set upon,
and he muddies all bright colors to dull brown.

I sometimes see the river by which I might
cross to the realm of virtue and, once there,
feel peace and contentment at least now and then.

But an irresistible force comes from somewhere
to drive me back so that, in my sorry plight,
I learn to accept the death that awaits all men.

179

Geri,* whenever my sweet foe feels wrath
in her great pride the way she sometimes does,
I cling to one comforting thought because
it helps me negotiate my difficult path:

when she turns her eyes in an angry glare at me
as if she were about to take the light
out of my life and leave me in endless night,
I stare back in my abject humility,

and she relents. If she didn't I would no more
seek her out than I would want to stare
at Medusa whose hair could petrify her poor

victims. I urge you then, do not despair.
You cannot flee, which I'm afraid is your
alternative: Love follows everywhere.

---

* Geri Gianfigliazzi, a poet of Florence, who had sent Petrarch a sonnet.

180

Here I am on the Po that can carry my
outer shell on its current toward the sea,
but my spirit can ignore your force, run free
wherever it chooses and, above you, fly.

He does not tack to port or starboard but goes
into the wind, steering toward his landmark
of that field of gold where he would disembark
and he never adjusts his sails and never rows.

You are the king of rivers, a deity
who greets the sun at dawn and to its light
adds your aura, enriching each field and tree,

and you carry my body downstream by your might
that my spirit can transcend to carry me
back where we started, a kindly water sprite.

181

Love wove a cunning snare of pearls and gold
hidden away in the grass under a bough
of the laurel that I love even if, somehow,
beneath its shadow my heart was sad and cold.

The bait he set was sweet and bitter as gall:
my fear mixed with desire, and to my ear
came trilled notes from the air, gentle and dear,
unheard by anyone since Adam's fall.

There was light on every side that made the sun
seem dim, and she controlled the deadly snare
with hands whiter than ivory or snow.

I fell into that trap and am held there
by her grip on the net that Love has spun
and my desire that never lets me go.

182

Love turns up the heat of my heart with zeal
but then he cools it down again with fear
and between these extremes my mind will veer,
unable to tell which of them is real.

I shiver with chills and burn with feverish sweats
and my breath is short from fright and then desire.
I'm like some ladies who suddenly perspire
at a certain age, going through these upsets.

The worse pains are the hot flashes when I
burn both night and day and suffer the sweet
moments of torture that I am favored by.

These sudden awful raptures of mine defeat
my powers of description. I think to fly
up toward her but in vain my wings beat.

183

If a mere passing glance of hers can at once
reduce me to a helpless quivering thing,
or her words, so soft and comforting, can bring
light and life to my soul more than the sun's,

what if by blunder or ill luck I give
unintended offense so that she takes
the pity from her lovely eyes and makes
a moue of displeasure, how on earth shall I live?

That is why I tremble at her least
change of expression on which my life depends
and by which my hopes are diminished or increased.

Women, we know, are labile, but she sends
me soaring or crashing. It is famine or feast.
And men's passion, strong as it may be, ends.

184

Nature, Love, and that sweet, modest soul
in which all virtues congregate and preside
conspire against me. Love plans a homicide
swift and merciless—his usual goal.

Nature sustains my soul, if only just,
and it is feeble and wretched and can bear
no blows or buffets, languishes in despair
and wishes it were free of its mortal dust.

I fail hour by hour without any slight
hope of a reprieve from that loveliness
whose poison I have learned to hunger for.

Unless Pity arrives and decides to fight
with Death for me, my prospects are ever less
sanguine. I cannot struggle anymore.

185

Behold the phoenix with its feathers of gold
that encircle the graceful white of its long neck
as if nature had come in homage to bedeck
with bijouterie that is neither bought nor sold.

A rarity, it lights the atmosphere
as Love's flint strikes the sparks that glint within,
and from the liquid fire that has been
kindled, all hearts are warmed of those who are near.

With a dress of scarlet trimmed in the blue of the sky
and a shawl embroidered with roses that wraps around
her shoulders, she is beauty's embodiment.

We hear that the phoenix has its home on a high
peak in the eastern mountains' untrodden ground,
but when it chooses can deign to make a descent.

186

If Homer and then Virgil had ever seen
the sun that shines upon me, they would have known
that warfare has its place, but love alone
is of all the verse forms surely the queen.

Aeneas, Achilles, Ulysses, and all those brave
warriors and demigods who fought
for Agamemnon, or against, we ought
to study, but love is what we truly crave.

Ennius wrote of Scipio's defeat
of Carthage and his valor in the war,
but I think if his star were shining now

it would prompt a song more gentle and more sweet,
the kind of poem I am aiming for
to praise my Lady, if she will allow.

187

When at Achilles' tomb Alexander arrived,
we are told he sighed as he addressed the dead
hero. "O lucky man!" is what he said,
"to have found a poet through whom you have survived!"

And yet this exquisite dove the like of whom
has not been seen in this world has only me,
lacking in style and grace and energy,
to attempt to rescue her from eternity's gloom.

She deserves at least a Homer or a divine
Orpheus, or perhaps the Mantuan bard*
to celebrate her grace as she walks on earth.

What a mixed blessing that this task should be mine—
I adore her, but for all my high regard,
my praise cannot begin to describe her worth.

---

* Virgil.

188

O sun, the source of all life, the one tree
I love, you have loved, too, and her equal has
not been seen on earth since Adam was
in that sweet place where we all yearn to be.

Let us pause to admire her. You run
away and darken the hillsides in the west,
taking from me what I like the best
in all the world. Yet stay awhile, dear sun!

The shadow falls even from that small hill
underneath which my modest fire glows
and where from a delicate sapling this tree grew . . .

and as I speak, the shadow is spreading still,
obscuring the best of all the world's tableaux
where my Lady lives and where my heart lives, too.

189

My scow with its heavy load is riding low;
oblivion is the cargo; the waves are rough;
and if Scylla and Charybdis weren't enough,
my foe at the tiller chooses where we go.

Each oar is manned by some capricious notion
that takes no note at all of seas and skies,
the torrents of tears, or the gusts of endless sighs
that tatter the sails as we plow through the ocean.

There are thick mists of hatred, and the lines,
soaked and slick, are tangled with carelessness
while with roll and pitch and yaw we wallow through

the treacherous water, and all of this combines
to obscure the stars that might give hope of success
even with this clumsy and ignorant crew.

190

Before me there appeared a snow-white doe
with golden horns, between two flowing streams
beside a laurel, just as in my dreams,
on a springtime day when the green buds seem to glow.

Her look was at the same time proud and kind
and I put everything by to follow her,
a miser seeking treasure, as it were,
and for whom gold is always on his mind.

Around her neck a jeweled choker said:
"Do not touch me! I am, by Caesar's grace,
free to wander safely as I please."

It was noon and the sun was already overhead
as I approached her in that sacred space,
but then she turned and vanished into the trees.

191

As the joy of the afterlife is in gazing upon
the face of God and wanting nothing more
(what could one want?), so, Lady, standing before
your face on earth is my eternal dawn.

And I have never seen you looking better
than at this moment of this blessed hour
and I find myself entirely in your power
in a bliss in which nothing else in life can matter.

If only this could last I would not ask
for anything more. Some beings live on air
and some, it is said, sustain themselves with fire,

while some need only water. For me to bask
in delight in seeing you is my needful fare
and the sweet fulfillment of my one desire.

192

Let us pause, Love, to consider these great
splendors, beyond what Nature could have made
alone—the amazing sweetness that is arrayed
in a heavenly light for the earth to contemplate.

What masterly skill has finished with gold and strewn
pearls on the roseate flesh as never before,
so that her feet moving across the floor
enrapture the cloistered hills in the afternoon.

The green grass and the wildflowers of bright
hues beneath the leaves of stately oaks
entreat her feet to favor them with her weight;

there are sparks above her as on a starry night,
and rejoicing everywhere that she provokes
and that her simple passing by can create.

193

My mind feeds upon such noble food
that I have no need of Jove's ambrosia or
Olympian nectar. Just gazing suffices for
an oblivion equal to that of Lethe's flood.

I hear her words and write them in my heart
so I can refer to them again and sigh,
transported, but not knowing how or why,
to a paradise I glimpse only in part.

That voice, delighting Heaven, utters phrases
so charming and words of such pure grace that one
who has not heard for himself how she amazes

could never imagine how under the sun
there could be this Art and Wit. My inadequate praise is
a disfigurement, I fear, even worse than none.

194

The noble breeze that sweeps away the night
mists and calls forth flowers in woods and hills
I recognize as the same soft breath that fills
my soul with ambition and makes me want to write.

To find a place where my heart and mind could rest
I fled my home and beloved Tuscan air,
looking for light and searching for calm somewhere
that I could address my task and do my best.

But the light I have still emanates from her
and Love is prompting me at once to return,
although I am dazzled and can hardly move.

Having no need of armor, I'd prefer
wings, but Heaven begrudges me, and I yearn
to be transported by magic or by Love.

195

Day by day, my face changes and hair
fades to tell me that I am too old for this.
The bait on the hook grows notional and is
mere habit now. The laurel branch is bare

on which there's lime to trap me. The sea will lose
its water, and the stars above burn out
before I am done with my desire and doubt,
which, at my age, are harder to excuse.

But until I am plucked and cleaned and torn apart
or until my enemy shows me pity, I
shall not desist in this impossible quest.

Unlikely things could happen, however: my heart
could stop for death or another woman by
whom I might be cured or laid to rest.

196

The breeze that touches my face in its serene
passage through the greenery reminds
me of Love's first assault and finds
me bearing still that wound as I have been

ever since. It recalls for me her face,
never clouded with disapproval or
jealousy, and her hair that I adore
braided with gems and pearls to hold it in place.

Sometimes she shakes it free and with her hand
in a lovely gesture I can never resist
fluffs it back, while I find that the band

holding my heart is tightening like a fist.
I cannot free myself nor can I withstand
the pressure that until my death will persist.

197

The celestial breeze caressing the laurel's green
boughs where Love once struck Apollo's side
has yoked my neck and I am mortified
without my freedom as I have so long been.

Atlas, in the desert, saw the face
Perseus showed him of Medusa and he
was changed into a mountain. But look at me—
also bewitched and in as sorry a case.

Medusa's hair was snakes, while hers is gold,
but it ties me, hand and foot, body and soul,
and struggling binds me tighter, as I have learned.

Her passing shadow can turn my heart ice-cold
and my face goes white with fear when the glowing coal
of her angry eyes turns toward me and I am burned.

198

From the air's golden shimmer Love spins a strong
but delicate cord to bind my helpless heart,
slender as a single hair but his art
in holding me as his captive makes it strong.

The marrow in my bones, the blood in my veins
jells and trembles whenever we meet, for she
on her fragile scale weighs life and death for me,
held captive as I am in these gossamer chains.

What can I say? Two dazzling lights that shine
show me the complex knots on my left and right
that I cannot figure out, let alone undo.

My mind baffled, my body bound, I refine
the definition of torment, caught in the light
of those beautiful eyes that freeze me in her view.

199

Oh, lovely hand, your grasp of my heart is tight
and in such a small space you confine my life
in which Heaven and Nature in constant strife
for glory collaborate by day and night!

Oh, fingers white as any pearl, you are sweet
but bitter only to me as they press upon
my open wound (but once the pain is gone,
I feel fulfilled and my happiness is complete).

The glove she wears conceals the flawlessness
of the ivory and rose of the delicate
hand within, the finest hand on earth.

I cannot see through its veil but have to guess
at the treasures it hides, amazing and exquisite,
exceeding the ransom of any king in worth.

200

Not just the one elegant hand that is clad
in a glove but the other also, and they bring
themselves together and with their arms they wring
the heart within my chest and drive me mad.

Love spreads a thousand snares and they succeed
in trapping me with the chaste, irresistible bait
of her speech and gestures, her poised and graceful gait
upon which my eyes, as if they were starving, feed.

I think of the sweep of her brows about her serene
eyes, and of her angelic rosebud lips
from which come soft sweet words I dote upon.

Her tresses have an iridescent sheen
brilliant enough to dazzle and even eclipse
at high noon in the summertime the sun.

201

Love and Luck together presented me
with a silken cloth embroidered all over with gold
thread, a joy in my rough hand to hold
for it had been hers, as it would always be.

In an instant I was rich and I was poor,
having this but not having her, and shame
and anger mixed in me as well in the same
proportions, so I was worse off than before.

I should have held it tightly and with more force
for I could have overcome an angel, small
and delicate. Or I had another course,

which would have been to flee from her hand and thrall
and the serious hurts they have done to me, far worse
because this was never her intention at all.

202

From ice as clear as crystal comes a fire
that kindles me and melts me. Then I dry,
diminished drop by drop, until I die
leaving only an odor of desire.

An angry Death has raised her arm to strike
and a wrathful heaven thunders ire, roaring
like a pride of lions, threatening and deploring:
I cower, never having heard the like.

Pity allied with Love might save me yet,
with forces arriving from two different directions
to intervene and fend off Death's assault.

But I have my doubts and I cannot forget
that stern glance of the mistress of my affections
that must have been, at least in part, my fault.

203

Alas, I burn, but the cause of my deep sighs
disbelieves what everyone else can see
plainly enough, and I think that even she
would admit, too, if she could trust her eyes.

Vast in beauty, in faith diminutive,
she declines to see through to my sad soul.
A very unlucky star must have control
of my destiny, if this is how I live.

My ardor that you hold in such low esteem
and my praises for you that these rhymes have professed
may spark other hearts than yours and set them afire.

It may well happen, as I sometimes dream,
that long after you and I have been laid to rest,
living readers will tremble with my desire.

204

Soul, you see so many things and hear
so much and read and speak and think, and write,
and you, senses, who bring me such delight
reporting her words and images so dear,

how strongly would you have wished that we were not
on this hard road we travel, that we had come
either sooner or later, and were free from
those footprints that we trace from spot to spot.

But here we are and we must not lose our way
on this brief journey to our eternal rest.
It is she who guides us so that we do not stray

and are never distracted from this sacred quest
toward Heaven. Although her mists of disdain may
trouble us, we'll give thanks for being blessed.

205

Sweet angers, sweet contempt, sweet moments of peace,
sweet bitterness, sweet torment, and sweet pain,
sweet speech of which I hear the sweet refrain
like a sweet breeze (but then the fires increase)!

But my soul must not complain. I must resign
myself to the sweet gall that has done us harm,
for there is honor in loving her and charm
in dreams in which I imagine her as mine.

Perhaps there will come a time when someone will say,
sighing in envy, "Look at this man's feat,
enduring so much for Love's laudable sake!"

And another will add to this in his dismay,
"Why was I deprived of the chance to meet
this woman? It is time's and fate's mistake."

208

Swift stream roaring from Alpine heights, you fall
carving your bed ever deeper as you go
in a passion that we have in common (although
I'm led by Love, but you by Nature's call):

roll on, for neither sleep nor weariness
can check your progress toward the beckoning sea,
but note how all around you one breathes free
in air that is all the fresher for your caress.

Look up in the sky to see the sun's bright rays
beflowering your bank and my life, too.
You are rapid while I'm a sluggish creek.

Be my emissary. For my delays
apologize to her as I would do,
for the spirit is most willing, but flesh is weak.

209

This sweet hill country where I put myself down,
having left behind what I cannot leave,
surrounds me with its charms that cannot deceive
my mind or distract my heart from what it has known.

I marvel how, at this great distance, I
can move and yet not move: the yoke remains
heavy on my neck and causes pains
from far away that I am afflicted by.

I am a deer with an arrow in my side
that the archer has poisoned, so that the faster I run
the more it hurts, and effort is nullified.

The arrow in me, however, is like none
other, for it delights me, so I have tried
to adjust to its sorrow as I have always done.

210

From Spain's Ebro to India's Hydaspes*
there is only the single phoenix, that unique bird:
none of us has seen it but all have heard
that it exists, the rarest of rarities.

I have only a crow and a raven to croak
the sad fate the Parcae† have spooled for me,
difficult, painful, and brimming with misery.
And Pity has turned a deaf ear to my joke.

I'd as soon not speak of her at all.
Whoever sees her feels his bosom fill
with love and sweetness, but this can turn to gall

when she does not deign to notice me, and a chill
seizes me. My hopes, my spirits fall,
and I am suddenly white-haired, old, and ill.

---

* Probably the Jhellum River.
† The three Fates.

211

Willpower spurs me, Love directs me, and pleasure
tugs at me, while custom drives me on.
Hope revives my spirits, almost gone,
and renews my courage with help beyond all measure.

I grasp at straws and manage to ignore
how my unseeing and unfaithful guide
is not an ally and does not take my side,
while reason suggests that I give up this war.

Sweet words, Virtue, and Honor have all conspired
to entangle me in this futile enterprise
in which I can foretell a dismal fate.

It was thirteen twenty-seven at sunrise
when I entered this labyrinth, and I am tired
and desperate and I cannot find the gate.

212

In a blessed dream, I languish and am content
with the shadows I embrace and the passing breeze.
I swim in an endless ocean and take my ease
floating, almost a part of its element.

I gaze up at the sun that has blinded me
with its unrelenting brightness. Now I pursue
a fleeing doe, as men in tapestries do,
but I ride on an ox slowed by infirmity.

Sightless, exhausted, what I fear I am seeking
is my own harm and through it my release
and I cry to Love, my Lady, and Death for aid.

After twenty years of this havoc-wreaking,
I cannot even remember my life of peace
before I was hooked and mercilessly played.

213

Graces that Heaven grants to very few
and virtues that are rare among humankind;
beneath the golden hair a sagacious mind;
modest but in her beauty godlike, too.

An ideal charm that is natural in her;
a singing voice hearing which all souls
melt; a delicate walk that is like a foal's;
and a spirit to which all other spirits defer.

Ah, and those eyes that can turn hearts to stone,
light up a dark abyss, make night like day,
and transport souls by spells that she has cast;

and her conversation, affable in tone
but full of insight; and gentle sighs that say
more than words . . . By these am I held fast.

215

All things combine, her noble blood, and yet
a life of modesty, great intellect
in a pure and innocent heart, which can reflect
with a wisdom that the features of youth offset.

She is the planet's ornament: her star
shines down, I swear, with praises for her worth
without a rival anywhere on earth—
my pen is poised but my mouth hangs ajar.

In her, Love has joined forces with chastity,
with natural beauty, a most attractive poise,
and gestures with which speech cannot compete.

There is something in her eyes—what can it be?—
that lights the night and dims the day, destroys
honey's sweetness, and makes the wormwood sweet.

216

All day I weep and then all night when we
mortals expect to find oblivion
if not repose. My tears are never done
but well up in my eyes from misery.

More than my eyes, my grieving heart is worn
to the edge of exhaustion. I am a pitiful thing
ever since I felt Love's arrow sting
my being and an object of men's scorn.

Sunrise to sunrise, dusk to dusk, I hurry
through a life that seems like death to me,
a nightmare I cannot fail to understand.

I grieve for someone else as well and worry
why she does not show any pity. She
sees my pain and will not lift a hand.

217

I wanted to write laments that would kindle a fire
of pity in her soul with meter and rhyme
to melt a heart that is icy in summertime
and that others might be moved by and admire,

and the force of my words would disperse the clouds that keep
her emotions chilly. Or at least the rest
of the world would learn of her and come to detest
her indifference that undoes me and makes me weep.

But no, I do not hate her and have no
pity for myself. It is my star
that brings me this fate. When my life is complete

the world will remember her beauty for I will show
my readers in these verses of mine that are
inadequate how my life and death were sweet.

218

In any group of graceful ladies, she
is the cynosure who does not have a near
rival, for they all but disappear
like stars in the daylight sky and are hard to see.

Love then seems to whisper in my ear,
"As long as she thrives, your lives will be
good, but after she passes on, I see
darkness and the end of my kingdom here.

"Think what the heavens would be where no moon shone;
imagine air without wind, or earth without grass;
or imagine man if language were unknown.

"Try to conceive of a vast ocean that has
neither fish nor waves. When Death on his throne
takes her, all of this will come to pass."

219

At daybreak plangent birdsong fills the air
that the hills and valleys echo, and the flow
of crystal brooks adds a continuo
in an aubade all the parts of nature share.

Aurora wakens, radiant and divine,
to perform a loving dance like that of light
on water, celebrating the end of night,
and she combs Tithonus's hair, snow-white like mine.

I am awake once more to salute the dawn,
the dazzling sun, and the other sun in my
heaven, lighting my way from youth and on

throughout my life. Sometimes, if only by
accident, they rise together and one
eclipses the other to rule alone in the sky.

220

From what secret mine did Love extract the pure
gold to make those tresses? From what lush
garden did he find the right rosebush
and the perfect rose for lips of such allure?

In what depths were those pearls with which she speaks
her sweet words that are irresistibly chaste?
What heights did he plunder for those charms he placed
on her elegant forehead, jaw, and perfect cheeks?

Which angel from what heavenly sphere brought here
her paradisiacal song that melts my soul
so that there is little of me that remains?

What gave such a special light to the atmosphere
that gleams from those lovely eyes and can control
war and peace, my weather, my losses or gains?

221

What sorry fate plays tricks on me to lead
me to a battlefield where I always lose?
I'll die or I'll be saved, and it's hard to choose
which is worse. To fail is to succeed.

These sparks have been in my heart for twenty years
sweetly tormenting so that I blaze anew
as I had supposed only young lovers do.
Will it ever subside? What are my hopes or fears?

I hear Death's menacing tread that follows her
footsteps, and the pain comes, and the balm.
Her gaze can strike like lightning and it can stir

my sluggish heart but not without a qualm
of fear. But to descibe how this can occur
requires a better poet than I am.

222

"Dear ladies all together, I ask you, where
is the one who is my life and my death as well?
Why is she not among you? Can you tell
me anything at all about how she may fare?"

"We're sad not to have her among us, but we
are also relieved, for she arouses in us
jealousy and envy: it's onerous
to be compared with her as we must be."

"But lovers, irrational, have no laws to guide them."
"True enough, and souls go where they will;
for bodies, Anger can be dispositive."

"But mark the faces of women when, beside them,
their suitors stand. They are beautiful but still
can weep at what they cannot bear or forgive."

223

The golden car of the sun dips into the sea
and the blue sky darkens to gray and then
to black as does my mind, which faces again
a bitter night of anguish and misery.

I rehearse my griefs to one who does not pay
attention and I quarrel with my fate
and with an indifferent world I have come to hate,
and Love, and her, and myself whom I betray.

I have no hope of sleep or even of rest
but only lamentation that lasts until dawn
and tears welling up from my soul to pour from my eyes.

At daybreak, although the gloom of the sky is gone,
mine intensifies within my breast
as I wait for another sun that fails to rise.

224

If faithfulness in love, an honest heart,
unflagging devotion, and expressing courteously
my longing, if my passion's chastity,
and my persistence as I play the part

of a lover, if having my thoughts clear on my face,
or mumbled in broken words that trail away
out of embarrassment, and if my gray
pallor is love's color in my sad case,

if loving someone else more than I love
myself, if sighs of anger and despair
mixed with a sweetness I dare not admit,

if either burning or freezing while thinking of
you, if Love distracts me, I think you bear
most of the blame for being the source of it.

225

Twelve ladies, lounging chastely on a small
ship—or say twelve stars around the sun—
I witnessed in an excursion that was like none
ever seen or heard of that I can recall—

not even the *Argo* that went to fetch the gold
fleece could compare to it, nor the barque from Troy
that brought the shepherd to Greece whose selfish joy
occasioned the ruinous war and griefs untold.

I saw them then in a triumphal car
with my Laura singing modestly and sweetly
and leading the procession, as of course she would.

It was no earthly sight. Such visions are
gifts of heaven. Intuiting completely
I realized what Typhis* understood.

---

* Helmsman of the *Argo*.

226

No solitary sparrow up in the eaves
was ever as lonely as I am, and no beast
lurking deep in the wood felt in the least
such sorrows as afflict a man who grieves

for his lady's absence. Weeping is my delight;
laughter is my woe; all food is swill;
the nights are agony I get through until
the dawn arrives bringing its different blight.

Sleep, as men say, is the brother of Death, and he takes
my cares away by which I remain alive,
for misery is now my only goal.

This green and happy land, these woods and lakes,
and fields where other men find joy and thrive
cannot relieve the bleakness within my soul.

227

O breeze, you move among those golden strands
of hair, and are moved by them, a miser who pours
from fist to palm the gold coins he adores
in a rapture in which he is at one with his hands.

You live among those wisps that are whips to me
stinging my body as blow after blow rains down,
but the pain is sweet, and though my face may frown
my heart and soul rejoice in ecstasy.

I think I have found her, but she remains far away.
I entertain some hopes, but they disappear
or abide to ridicule me as I replay

what I let myself think. Wind, you have nothing to fear
but can toy with her coiffure however you may,
while I can find no good excuse to come near.

228

With his right hand Love opened up my chest
on the left side where he planted a laurel tree
in my heart's loam with vivid greenery
of a brilliant hue no emerald could best.

My pen has plowed the ground and my copious tears
have watered it as if with a gentle shower.
The tree has grown and flourishes to tower
over the grove and whisper to the spheres.

Honor, virtue, talent, grace, and fame
have their roots here in this chaste loveliness
clothed in a celestial beauty, which is

a burden I'm glad to bear, however it came.
In my prayers I offer thanks and bless
my singular fortune and unrivaled bliss.

229

I used to sing, but now I weep instead,
and I take from the weeping just as much delight
because the cause is the same and can excite
my emotions: I follow wherever I am led.

From her I am equally grateful for mildness or
harshness, cruel gestures as well kind.
If she takes any notice of me, I do not mind
how or why but am always eager for more.

Let Love and Fortune and my Lady go on
treating me as they do, they cannot affect,
despite their vicissitudes, the joy I take.

Here on earth or after I am gone,
there is no nobler state. Who would expect
a blossom so sweet that so bitter a root could make?

230

For a long time I wept, but now I sing
because my sun no longer hides from me
and I can see Love, chastely and delicately
but with majesty, rule like a great, powerful king.

Like Noah, I had had to face a deluge
but of my own tears of hopeless love,
and without the prospect of any delivering dove
or ark in which I might find some refuge.

There was no glimpse in any direction of shore
and I thought all was lost and waited to die
the lingering death that fortune had in store,

but Pity sent me an olive branch and I
saw the weather clear as I'd prayed for—
so I could go on living or, anyway, try.

231

I never used to feel any envy for those
who had an easier path than mine in love,
for their thousand joys were not the equal of
a single pang that my Lady bestows.

But now, she has fallen ill. My sun is obscured
by so dark a cloud that all my light is lost,
and I am at sea where my barque is tempest-tossed,
with no relief in sight until she is cured.

O Nature, compassionate mother who can be
so cruel, with such conflicting motives you make
beautiful but fragile things that we

admire, but then, as if on a whim, you break
what we have loved. I ask the Lord how he
can allow the capricious liberties you take.

232

Anger conquered conqueror Alexander*
so that he was a lesser man than his father,
never mind that he said that he would rather
choose the artists worthy to do the commander.

Tydeus,[†] dying, gnawed on the skull of his foe,
Menalippus; Sulla, in fury, went blind
and then died, entirely out of his mind,
as Valentinianus did also.[‡]

Ajax, on his rampage, killed cattle and then
anyone he encountered, because of the shield
he thought should have been his but Odysseus got.

This anger threatens reasonable men
to their own hurt. The double-edged sword we wield
leads to shame and death more often than not.

---

* Alexander, son of Philip of Macedon, killed a friend in a drunken rage. The
artists he selected were Pyrgoteles, Lysippus, and Apelles (for marble,
bronze, and paint).
[†] Tydeus was one of the Seven against Thebes.
[‡] L. Cornelius Sulla died of "apoplexy," as did Valentinianus I.

233

Those glorious eyes were darkened by her pain
that made mine dark as well, but from her right
eye came a glance that in that gloom was bright
and the significance of which, I think, was plain.

I had been waiting, hungering to see
the only one on earth for whom I care.
Heaven and Love, for the sake of my welfare,
deigned to show unusual kindness to me.

From her right eye to mine there came a ray
to cause a sickness that has joy as its
symptom. It flew from her to me, as I say,

like a heavenly body in one of its rare transits
to save me and to demonstrate the way
that there can be hope beyond the end of my wits.

234

This little room was once my refuge from
the hurts of the day's adventures, but now I weep
and tears pour down all night here, where I keep
the painful vigil every night has become.

In this little bed, I used to be able to rest,
comfort my pains, and recover from the blows
of the world, but my poor body no longer knows
a moment's peace. Tormented and distressed,

I flee seclusion, rest, and myself, too,
and every thought of her that brings me grief
in a nightmare from which there seems to be no waking.

Now I seek crowds and company, people who
distract me if they cannot bring relief.
It is hard to be alone when my heart is breaking.

235

Alas, it is Love who leads me beyond the bounds
of what is permissible, so that I offend
the queen of my heart as I could never intend
to do or for her complaints give any grounds.

No helmsman ever steered his ship with more
care with a rich cargo in the hold
than I maneuver, avoiding the rocks of her cold
looks that accuse me of being an oaf or a boor.

My vessel is all but swamped by torrents of tears
or capsized by repeated gale-force sighs
in the depths of wintertime in the dark of night.

Despite myself I provoke laughter or sneers
on a ruinous course I cannot rationalize.
My rudder is gone and there is no land in sight.

236

Love, that I'm doing wrong I am well well aware
but I cannot help myself. I act as though
I had lost my power of reason behaving so
shamefully whenever she is there.

Once I could curb my hot desire and hold
back to keep from beclouding her lovely face.
But you've seized the reins from my hands and now we chase
after her, and we're desperate and therefore bold.

My soul runs wild because of what you do
and, knowing no limits in its heated state,
behaves in ways that do not bear review

in pursuit of my Lady and willing to perpetrate
heinous crimes. But it is she and you
who incite me, and she should commiserate.

238

A royal nature, an angelic intellect,
a radiant soul, the eyes of a lynx, keen
and piercing, the gift of foresight, and a serene
character that in kings one may expect,*

he comes, and a bevy of lovely ladies are here
on this festive day to celebrate his visit.
He notices among them one exquisite
face in that large group that has no peer.

He waves the others away and summons this
perfect beauty to come and stand by his side
where he bestows upon her brow a kiss

in which the other girls and women take pride,
while I feel a sudden surge of envy for his
sweet gesture that leaves us all wide-eyed.

---

* The sonnet commemorates the visit Charles of Luxembourg to Avignon
  in 1346.

240

I have begged Love before and do so again
to urge you to pardon me for my offenses,
sweet pain, dear bane, for whom I leave my senses
pursuing what I cannot hope to obtain.

Reason, which should be sovereign of the soul
is often overpowered by Desire,
who pulls us down while we think we're climbing higher,
and, helpless, I have lost all self-control.

You have a heart that Heaven itself makes bright,
a clear mind, and virtue without flaw,
all but unmatched in our brief, earthly sojourn,

and you should understand my awkward plight
and how your presence fills me with helpless awe,
for your dangerous beauty makes my desire burn.

241

That haughty lord from whom we cannot hide
and against whom there is no defense pierced me
with his arrow of desire that immediately
brought upon me a pain that gratified,

but to that shaft of love he added a second
of pity to further his work so that I bestow
tears upon the altar of your woe
upon which, as a lover, I had not reckoned.

Your state elicits from my soul the heat
of fire as well as the cooling water of tears.
But these do not cancel each other out.

Rather they join together and, as it appears.
intensify my ardor while they compete
to make my prayers for your sake more devout.

242

"You see that little hill,* dear heart, it was there
that we left her, who sometimes deigned to pay,
if only out of pity, attention. Today
we weep a lake of tears in our despair.

"Go back there. I am resigned to being alone.
See if her mood is changed and we may end
this constant mourning, my partner and inner friend,
and our grief that has intensified and grown."

"You forget yourself, sir. I am not here
but have already left you, although you address
me yet. Can you not feel that your chest is hollow?

"You breathe, speak, and walk about, but I fear
your life is elsewhere and in your distress
you search for me and wish that you could follow."

---

* Generally believed to be Caumont, Laura's birthplace. See 243.

243

Fresh, shady, and ever-flowering hill
where she sits, sometimes singing or deep in thought,
providing us a glimpse of the heaven she ought
to reside in and one day assuredly will,

my heart that has wished to leave me and to dwell
with her (and I understand its inclination)
now goes searching for every indentation
her foot has made on what should be asphodel.

He blames me for not pausing for a while
in reverence, remarking, "The wretch is tired
of life, and dying here would show some style."

She smiles? But it is as if I have expired,
my heart having been removed, and in this vile
world, she is the paradise I've desired.

244*

The burden of my ills is heavy and I
fear even worse to come, for the prospect is
dismaying—of our howling in madness's
clutches with wrongs we cannot rectify.

Should I pray for peace or war? I do not know.
Our losses are great as is the shame we feel.
We're obliged to play the hand that the Fates deal
as we live out the destinies they bestow.

I do not deserve the honor that you pay me
and suppose it is because Love has distracted
you and clouded your judgment, but even so

I am grateful, wish you well, and hope you may be
stoic, aiming at heaven in these protracted
trials, remembering where we hope to go.

---

* A reply to a poem from Giovanni dell' Orologio, a physician.

245

Two fresh roses picked in Paradise
two days ago, on Mayday, a perfect cadeau
from an old lover to younger ones who know
what sweet speech does, and smiles, and flashing eyes

to gentle a savage beast and civilize
him in an instant, changing his hard heart
to softness as he learns the lover's art
from one who through long practice has grown wise.

"The sun has never seen a better pair
of lovers," he said, and smiled and gave a sigh
as he handed them the flowers and turned away.

My heart is weary, but for a moment there,
the flagging faith was revived that I live by.
Oh, happy couple! Oh, delightful day!

246

That gentle breeze that moves among the swaying
boughs of the laurel and through her golden hair
also transports men's souls through the air
so they leave the bodies in which they had been staying.

In a world of cruel thorns a pure white rose . . .
Who could imagine such a miraculous thing?
It is the glory of earth, and I beg of the king
of heaven that I die before she goes.

That will avoid my having to witness the great
blight that will come to the world, the loss of its light
and the general ruin that I anticipate,

for she has been the very lamp of my sight.
In the absence of her words, the world's fate
is the deathly silence of a perpetual night.

247

Some may doubt me and think my words of praise
for her are excessive, hyperbolic, and false,
claiming that she is more noble than anyone else,
more lovely, wiser, and charming in so many ways,

but the opposite is true: my reports are too
modest, and her virtues deserve much higher
celebration. One who may require
proof should meet her himself and form his own view.

Then he'd say, "What this man hopes to do
would be beyond the powers of Cicero
and Demosthenes, or Homer and Virgil, who

reached the limits of mortal powers that no
one has ever surpassed. Love draws him to
the impossible, and he knows that this is so."

248

Whoever wishes to see what Nature is
capable of, and Heaven, let him gaze
upon her, bask in her sun's brilliant rays
and behold what is beyond analysis.

Let him come quickly, for, as we know, Death
takes all, but takes first the fairest and best.
Heaven, where she will find eternal rest,
is eager for her arrival and holds its breath.

If he comes in time, he'll see all virtues met
in the one woman, with beauty and regal mien,
so splendid that he'll criticize my rhyme

and its efforts to describe the woman and yet
omitting so much that can be plainly seen.
But let him come quickly, not wasting any time.

249

I still feel fear, remembering the day
I departed from my Lady, who looked sad.
I left my heart behind but I am glad
my memory is vivid of the way

she stood there like a rose among wildflowers
outshining all the other ladies, stoic
or at least concealing her feelings in a heroic
effort that would be beyond my powers.

There was nothing special about the clothes she wore
and she was without her jewels of wit and laughter
so that I sensed that something was not right.

I left her there, but as I closed the door,
I worried that something dreadful might thereafter
happen. I pray that it was a baseless fright.

250

In dreams I used to gaze at her from afar
but it was she, and I took consolation
from her being present: now the situation
is changed and I worry what her troubles are.

On her dear face, I note the signs of pain
that she accepts with a sweet tranquillity
I cannot share. It troubles me to see
her suffer, and on her behalf I complain.

"Do you not recall that evening when
we were last together? I turned away
but still I noticed upon your cheek a tear.

"I did not tell you then, but now I say
you must not hope to see me ever again
upon this earth. My time is finished here."

251

Horrible dream! Dreadful vision! True?
Could she before her time be taken away,
my rock, my hope, my sorrow, my mainstay
in life, the purpose for all I say and do?

If it is true, would I not have heard at least
a rumor of such dreadful news that I
could use for confirmation? How and why
could God let his creation be so decreased?

I hope it turns out that her health is good
and that I shall see again what I live for—
that face I cherish, as the whole world should.

But if that vision of mine was something more
than fear and she moves on to angelhood,
I hope that my death, too, is soon in store.

252

In a dubious state I sing or else I weep.
I hope, I fear, or both at the same time.
I try to distract myself sometimes with rhyme,
but I am in Love's dungeon, dark and deep.

And she, the light by whom I steer and take
my bearings, she is nowhere to be seen.
I have no clear idea what this could mean.
Is there nothing in my future but heartbreak?

Will heaven collect on what we owe it or heed
the prayers of men on earth who will be undone
with our sun plucked from the sky so that we plead

for light, for vision. She is our very sun,
of which in this dark world we have great need.
What will become of us if she is gone?

253

Sweet glances, endearing little phrases,
when shall I ever see or hear you again?
Or those beautiful golden tresses of hers, when
shall I behold them and offer them my praises?

I am robbed of them all by implacable Fate
for which I weep and shall continue to do.
It used to be pleasure I sought but never knew
that it brought me pain, which now is my constant state.

I had some glimpses, there is no denying,
of her gentle eyes where my thoughts dwell, but then
after an instant of sweetness, I had to go

on some task I couldn't avoid in the world of men
over land and sea. It is not satisfying,
but yearning is the only loving I know.

254

No word, but is that good news or is it bad?
I have no idea what silence means of my
sweet enemy I am enchanted by,
and conflicting fears and hopes are driving me mad.

Beauty such as she has does not fare
well in this world, and she is lovelier far
than any I know and chaste, and the heavens are
understandably eager to welcome her there

as a star or, even better, a brilliant sun.
But if that happens, what will become of me?
My troubles will end, but my life will be done

and only a husk of myself, a nullity
will wander about with little purpose or none,
in pathetic premature senility.

255

Happy lovers wish for evening and hate
the dawn that draws their raptures to a close.
For me, the evening only refreshes my woes,
and morning is when my miseries abate.

Sometimes in the sky not one but two
suns appear in the resplendent east
to dazzle the skies with the light thus increased
and stun Heaven that stares down at the view

as happens in the springtime when earth turns
a vivid green. The roots of trees grow
deep, as do those of the love that in me burns.

Opposing, morning and evening sway me so,
but the latter brings on pain, and a wise man learns
to prefer the distractions that the dawns bestow.

256

I wish I could be avenged somehow for the way
her gaze and speech destroy me, but then she flees
and hides herself away so that I miss these
delights that also fill me with dismay.

She saps my spirits and wears me down like a beast
on the track of some slower, helpless game.
I hear her lion roar and am filled with shame
for she is about to make my heart her feast.

Death is about to evict my soul, which goes
away to pay a visit to her who is
the threat and the cause of all my many woes.

I have often tried to imagine this
encounter when my soul disturbs her repose:
does she hear or somehow guess what is amiss?

257

My eyes were full of desire and had fixed
on her fair face for which I longed so long,
but Love, correcting me, said I was wrong,
putting another wonder, her hand, betwixt

her face and me. To this I should have paid more
attention and homage. Now, I am hooked like an eel,
or caught like a limed bird, and the yearning I feel
has a new direction for me to take and explore.

I have a new dream, or another avenue
by which to approach, at least in dreams, my goal
without which nothing matters to me, a new

delight and torment, for now within my soul,
new joys compete with the old as I pursue
a novel strangeness that is familiar, too.

258

From those lovely eyes there came bright sparks she cast
in my direction, warming my heart, and sighs
as well as her sweet speech, a welcome surprise,
for her harshness, it appeared, had changed at last.

The memory of that moment occupies
my mind and I think how I nearly fainted away
in my gratitude and happiness that day
when I saw my dismal prospects begin to rise.

I had learned to put up with pain by which
I had been nursed, but now, beyond belief,
I had to accept the pleasure I could not trust.

Caught between fear and hope, at a fever pitch,
I questioned both the simplicity of relief
and the joy to which I could not quite adjust.

259

I have always preferred a life of solitude,
as the streams, woods, and meadows can testify,
to avoid the blind and deaf who have put by
all thought of Heaven after this interlude.

This I have found far from the fragrant air
of the Tuscany I love, in these dark hills
by the banks of the River Sorgue, which spills
from the Vaucluse, and I sing or I weep there.

But Fortune, who is always my sworn foe,
sends me to Avignon, where I am irate
to see the pride and waste and fecklessness.

All I've been spared is my hand and pen, which know
how to get by but not capitulate,
as my Lady knows, and I do, too, I confess.

260

I saw two lovely eyes that were brimming full
of chastity and sweetness, and this was
under a lucky star, and my heart has
learned to scorn all others in charm's school.

Has anyone ever lived who can compare
with her? Surely not the famous "face
that launched a thousand ships" and brought disgrace
to Greece and to high Troy blood everywhere.

Not honest Lucrece, who took her own
life after Tarquin raped her; nor Priam's fair
daughter Polyxena; nor Hypsipyle;

nor beautiful Argia.* She stands alone,
Nature's triumph, unprecedented, rare,
our moment's crowning glory—only she.

---

* The women are Helen; Lucrece; Polyxena, whom Achilles loved; Hypsipyle,
whom Jason seduced; and Argia, wife of Polynices (Oedipus's son).

261

Should any lady desire lasting fame
for wisdom or for virtue or social grace,
let her seek them in my enemy's face,
the home of all these qualities I name.

Let her learn honor and piety,
observe how chastity can combine with fun,
and see how Heaven's gate is open to one
who has such poise and stateliness as she.

There she will study speech and the even finer
art of silence; she will encounter a mind
more subtle than my poor wit can suggest.

But her beauty does not come from her design or
art: it is of a wholly spontaneous kind,
a gift of Nature, which is by far the best.

262

"Most precious is life," Laura's mother explained,
"and second is virtue." The daughter answered her,
"You have the order wrong. There never were
things still precious if their virtue was stained.

"Any woman who loses her honor is not
a woman anymore. She may look the same
but she is mortified by a sense of shame
far worse than any death, a fatal blot.

"I never questioned the action of Lucrece,
except that she used a knife. I would have thought
her anguish would have sufficed and her duress."

The philosphers' debate will never cease,
and we will study what we have been taught:
her heavenward ascent will be effortless.

263

Triumphal tree,* the poet's crown and that
of emperors, how deeply I have been
devoted to you and to your namesake in
our passage through this earthly habitat.

Her only goal and guide in living is
honor, which she most prizes and she earns.
Love's traps and wiles she naturally spurns,
immune to the machinations that are his.

For nobility of blood or rubies and gold
that the world values, she does not care at all
knowing how they are accidents of fate.

Her beauty would pain her, if the truth be told,
except that it can set off to no small
advantage her chaste and honorable state.

---

* The laurel.

265

A proud and savage heart that dwells in so
beautiful a body . . . How can I
resist? Helpless, I am defeated by
the combination, undone, and brought low.

I look to nature and see how flowers and grass
spring up only to die, how the light will fade,
giving way to night's oncoming shade
in the grim procession in which all things pass.

I live, nevertheless, on hope, aware
that over time with perseverance they say
dripping water can wear away a stone.

Her heart is not so cold that tears and prayer
cannot warm it a little day by day,
for it is mortal flesh and like my own.

266

My dear lord,* my thoughts are constantly of you
and your generous face, which I always keep in mind.
Fortune, on the other hand, less kind,
batters me, frustrating whatever I do.

My life is devoted to you and of course to her,
from whom, respectively, I receive pleasure and pain
that cause me to give my thanks or else to complain,
and I cannot even remember which I prefer.

The chains I have forged and fashioned link by link
are those of loyalty and love in a green
meadow with a column† and laurel tree.

I have been graced by both of these, I think,
for eighteen years with her, and with you fifteen,
and in my heart is this bright, indelible scene.

---

* Giovanni Cardinal Colonna, Petrarch's patron and friend.
† "Column," in Italian, is, of course, *colonna,* and the play on Laura and laurel
   we have seen often.

267*

Alas, that lovely face with its gentle gaze
and that elegant posture as she seemed to glide
rather than walk, and her speech where the least aside
could inspire the commonest men to try to amaze!

And that smile of hers that launched the dart at me
from Love's quiver that has been my great
joy! And that soul one might associate
with empresses from antiquity!

Of all these we are now deprived and I
mourn my loss, the worst I can conceive,
that leaves me in irreparable despair.

You were my hope, my dream, and it was by
your leave I lived. I cannot quite believe
that your words are lost, vanished into the air.

---

* News of Laura's death reached Petrarch on May 19, 1348.

269

The column is fallen* and the green laurel tree
is down under the shade of which I found
respite from my cares. Now on bare ground
is a lifeless glare that extends from sea to sea.

Death has robbed me twice of what I held
dearest in the world and cannot be
replaced by land, wealth, or nobility—
a double loss that is unparalleled.

If this is destiny's will, what can I do
but let my soul learn sadness and my eyes
tears as I make my slow way through

a life I thought was nearly paradise?
But all that has disappeared in a moment or two
and I must adjust to catastrophic surprise.

---

* Cardinal Colonna died on July 3, 1348.

271

The burning knot that held me for twenty-one
years has been at last untied by Death.
My sorrow is such as to take away my breath—
and yet I breathe as I have always done.

Love has not given up but has set a new
snare to trap me, lighting another fire
he supposed would grow, increasing my desire
in the difficult time that I was going through.

Had I not learned from my earlier trials, I should
have been his prey and suffered those pains again,
weeping as I used to do in the dark,

for my heart, as he suspected, was now dry wood.
But Death had dragged me back to the world of men
cutting Love's knot and extinguishing every spark.

272

Life skips on by and does not pause to rest,
while Death, relentless, pursues with heavy strides.
I, meanwhile, am assaulted on all sides
by past and future, their malice manifest

as memory and desire together sit
upon my heart, mocking my life, while I
cannot move them or think how to reply,
deficient in spirit, energy, and wit.

I used to have some clear notion of why
I did this or that and even would ignore
ominous skies that ought to have cautioned me.

The squalls have come even so, and the sea and sky
churn and rage. I despair of reaching shore,
while the stars above hide in obscurity.

273

What are you up to? Thinking? You keep on turning
your mind to the past and things that cannot change.
Poor soul! Do you not at least admit it is strange
to pile wood on the fire from which you're burning?

Those sweet words and those gentle looks that are all
gone from the earth forever . . . It does no good
for you to remember them in detail and brood
or mourn, or even in detail to recall.

You need another kind of enterprise
to which you can turn your thoughts, a better way
to spend your time. Why not raise your eyes

to heaven where all beauties and virtues stay
incorruptible? If you are wise,
you'll learn from the deep grief you feel today.

274

Peace, I beg you! My own thoughts attack.
As if Love, Death, and Fortune without aid
were not enough, I find myself betrayed
by inner foes that stab me in the back.

And you, my heart, you are a traitor, too!
You make your pacts with those who torment me
as if you wished somehow to be set free
even before my days on earth are through.

You carry messages from Love, and in you
Fortune holds her court with pomp and show.
Each heartbeat brings me closer to my grave.

I struggle with you and my errant thoughts as I go
step by cautious step as fugitives do,
pretending, despite you both, that I am brave.

275

Poor eyes of mine, our sun has been obscured,
ascending into the higher realms of the air
to shine still, although we can't see it there.
Does it wait for us? Is our arrival assured?

Poor ears, the words you are accustomed to hear
resound still for those who are close by.
Poor feet, you can no longer satisfy
my longing to approach her and come near.

Why do you all revolt against me so?
Her absence is not my fault. You must put the blame
on Death, or you can praise the Lord: although

his wisdom is hard to understand, He came
to offer eternal life to us below,
whose grief and joy one day will be the same.

276

Her disappearance has plunged my fragile soul
into darkest sorrow and even fear:
it is not for any comfort, let alone cheer,
but I write to clarify and perhaps condole.

I have every right to complain, as Love knows well,
for it and she were my heart's only balm,
my single source of fortitude and calm
in a life that otherwise would have been hell.

But Death has robbed me, and happy Earth has received
her lovely face and has covered it away.
I am left diminished and aggrieved,

blinded and in despair. My light of day
is gone and cannot ever be retrieved
in a gloom unbroken by even the faintest ray.

277

If Love does not come up with some new plan
I may trade in my disagreeable life,
full of sorrow, fear, heartbreak, and strife,
for something more congenial to a man

who, although hope is gone, still feels desire.
My days and nights are filled with sighs and tears.
My vessel yaws and pitches as it careers
through shoals where waves break higher and ever higher.

I must find a pilot, for mine is gone,
laid in the earth or promoted to the skies
in which she shines, a star or another sun

that my heart can see clearly but not my eyes.
I cannot peer through the veil I wear, which is one
that grief and age together improvise.

278

At the very peak of her beauty, when Love has
his greatest power, she abruptly left
us all who are still here behind, bereft,
and the earth itself diminished from what it was,

ascending to Heaven where she rules and draws
my strength and will upward. Existence here
is otiose, though I take a modest cheer
hoping to see her after the briefest pause.

Do I deserve this? Will she intercede?
Can my soul follow hers and also rise?
Can I leave these woes I do not want or need,

the heavy burdens from which I wait to be freed?
Three years have now gone by since her demise,
a torment for the end of which I plead.

279

Some hear the cooing of mourning doves and the gentle
sounds of the breeze among the swaying reeds
or the whisper of the surf as it recedes
from the seashore that can seem to the sentimental

poignant: I sit alone here and I write,
hearing and seeing only her, whose worth
heaven has concealed beneath the earth
but who is yet the source of my delight.

"Why do you waste away like this before
your time has come?" she asks me. "Your sad eyes
still spill forth a stream of tears in your

grief for me, but you must realize
my day is now eternal and is more
bright than what one loses when he dies."

280

This is the nearly perfect place where I may
almost see the elusive vision that I
long for but the implacable fates deny,
if only because I want it so much and they

love to tease. But where else can I find
attractive caves and hollows in which to sigh?
Venus herself in Cyprus would envy my
valley of the Vaucluse that gives my mind

comfort. The brooks babble and the trees
whisper to birds and flowers in the grass
of love and its manifold felicities,

but you in heaven, contradicting these
temptations that the world of nature has
on offer, speak of joyful eternities.

281

How many times have I fled here not merely
from the madding crowd but myself insofar
as anyone can to a refuge where the severely
troubled may find in crepuscular

hideaways some solace? For the relief
that Death has snatched away from me I plead,
begging him to take me and my grief—
but he is obdurate and pays no heed,

so I summon her, and she appears to me
as a nymph coming out of the Sorgue to take a seat
on the riverbank where for a time I see

that longed-for face once more, gentle and sweet.
She is silent but gazes compassionately
upon me so that my heart skips a beat.

282

O blissful soul, how often do you return
to comfort me in my night miseries
with your eyes bright—Death has not dimmed these—
as lovely as ever in the way they burn.

How happy it makes me that you still appear
to gladden my heart that otherwise is so
bereft, bringing that beauty that I know
so well and deeply long to see down here.

I sing of you still and I wander the earth to recall
places where we were. I do not weep
for you, but for my loss do my tears fall.

The only comfort I can find at all
is in your apparitions here that keep
me sane and still have power to enthrall.

283

Death, you have discolored the loveliest
face there ever was and have vandalized
those beautiful eyes that I so dearly prized
as you freed her soul from her body laid to rest.

With but a single stroke you have beggared me
and silenced the sweetest voice that ever sounded
with gentle, intelligent words, so that I am wounded
by all lesser sounds I hear and things I see.

An occasional revenant, she comes to give
solace to one whose sorrow is so deep
that otherwise, I might not be able to find

the will to draw breath, but for her sake I keep
my heart beating and I contrive to live
as slag after its gold has been refined.

284

So fast the time passes and so quick
is the thought of my Lady that, even if she is dead,
my sorrows' anodyne pops into my head,
her gentle image—and I am no longer sick.

Love who has nailed me to his cross relents
at her approach: he is defeated by
her gentleness, and for that moment I
am whole again through her beneficence.

It is as if she had come home again
and her aura's shimmer drives away the gloom
that weighed my spirit down and filled my heart.

Unaccustomed to such brightness, then,
my soul is dazzled. "To heaven's anteroom
you light the way. I'm ready to depart."

285

Never did a mother give her son
or a pious wife, her loving husband such wise
counsel, offered sadly and with sighs,
in difficult times by which men are undone

as she has brought down to me from on high,
encouraging me or offering correction
and always in a spirit of affection
so that I am delighted to comply.

Her concern for me is written on her face
as she tells me what to avoid and what to pursue,
gently reminding me how much she cares.

Knowing that she waits for me, I do
better than my best, blessed by her grace
and by that feeling of peace her spirit shares.

286

Could I begin to suggest how the gentle breeze
I hear reminds my of my Lady's sighs
(She is in Heaven now, but if my eyes
can't see her, still I hear her among the trees),

or if I could describe this presence I feel,
it would move the hardest heart and mind.
So loving is she, so gentle and so kind
that only a churl would dare to doubt she's real.

She is my tutor, mentor, and my guide
urging me to do the right and just
thing, firmly and yet with a slight regret.

I have learned to conform to her will and trust
her judgment. She is always by my side,
murmuring wisdom I cannot forget.

287

Dear old Sennuccio,* you have flown, leaving
behind the body's prison but also your
friends, who take comfort as we reassure
ourselves that your soul is now beyond our grieving,

for you have ascended high enough to see
both poles at once and the whirling stars in the skies
and to understand the limits of mortal eyes.
Meanwhile we recognize that you are free.

Convey my respects, if you would, to your revered
colleagues in the third sphere—Dante, Cino,
Guittone, and Franceschino,† who appeared

here to show us the way. And let there be no
delay in greeting her to whom I adhered
in life and who has become my baldachino.

---

* Sennuccio del Bene, the poet and Petrarch's friend, died in 1349.
† Dante Alighieri, Cino da Pistoia, Guittone d'Arezzo, and Franceschini
degli Albizzi, all poets who were predecessors of Sennuccio and Petrarch.

288

I have filled the ambient air with sighs
as I looked from these hills to the gentle plain
where she was born and lived and where remain
her redolences that I still idolize.

She left us so abruptly that what I see
is a clear vacancy, a negative space,
which, if it were filled, would be her face
that used to light the whole vicinity.

There is on this hill neither shrub nor stone,
nor branch nor individual leaf or flower,
nor a single blade of grass nor trickling stream

nor savage beast that does not feel alone,
bereft, and diminished since that fatal hour
and does not share my melancholy dream.

289

My soul's flame, fairest of all the fair,
whom Heaven favored while she dwelt down here
has left us, far too soon, so she could appear
among the bright stars, belonging there.

I have recovered enough to realize
that she was right to put me off as she would.
I was importunate but she understood,
and even forgave with a glance of her downcast eyes.

I thank her now for her rebuffs that were
gifts of good counsel offered for my sake
to save me from the flames in which I burned

I would have risked worse flames if I did not take
those lessons into my heart I had from her
and profited by—as only now I have learned.

290

Times change, and what was a bother I
now understand was a blessing in disguise
with my pains nudging me toward paradise
as I struggled with what was meant to purify

my soul. Oh, my desires all those years
were wrong and false, as she well understood,
and for my sake and in order to do me good,
she ignored my sighs and my misguided tears.

Love had made me blind and deaf to all
reason, as I pursued the catastrophe
awaiting me. Now that she's gone I cherish

the memory of that generosity
with which she rescued me, about to fall
and through my own stupidity to perish.

291

At daybreak when I look up to admire
dawn with her rosy cheeks and golden hair,
I am seized again with passion for the fair
Laura and I feel the familiar fire.

How happy must Tithonus be who knows
the hour at which his beloved will return.
Having no such consolation, I burn
and long not for the day's but my life's close.

Their partings are not so painful: she comes back
every night to tousle his white hair
and renew their union, sweet and always the same.

My days are dull but my nights, too, are black:
I reach out, but I cannot embrace thin air
to which I try to speak, calling her name.

292

Those amazing eyes I've spoken about so often,
the arms, the delicate hands and feet, the face
that transformed me as well as my commonplace
life are gone, reduced to dust in a coffin.

Her angelic glance was like the lightning flash
when the strike is nearby, and it would light
the earth with heavenly glory, but the sight
is gone in an instant, before the thunder crash.

And I persist, which I find hard to bear,
depressing, infuriating, abandoned by
that light I lived for. It is no longer there,

nor is my accustomed wit. I find that I
am without words and, worse, that I don't care.
Abjuring them, I am content to sigh.

293

Had I but thought this canticle of sighs
would have been so well received, I'd have made
many more, and they would have displayed
more elegance before their readers' eyes.

But now that she's gone who prompted me to sing
and whom I hoped to please, I lack the heart
to improve, correcting each defective part
and making every verse a lovely thing.

What I hoped for then was relief from pain,
some moments of distraction, a way to vent
emotion. I was never thinking of fame.

That old persistent turbulence is spent,
and I wish I could please, for her sake, but in vain
do I labor, mute and weary. It's not the same.

294

She visited in my heart in much the same
way a great lady might for a day or two
stay in a country cottage, passing through.
She's gone, and I'm what I was before she came,

or worse, because I now have been stripped bare.
Love's torch has guttered out and lifelessness
fills the rooms. The house is a mere address,
a derelict building, and nobody lives there.

But inside there is weeping, although no ears
can hear it, and pain the dust can somehow feel.
And are those sighs or just the wind in the eaves?

If these are fancies, still the grief is real,
which turns a passing shower into tears.
An emptiness dwells here that breathes and grieves.

295

There was a conversation in my mind
of thoughts of her: "She may soon regret
her diffidence. She may feel pity yet.
Her thoughts of you are nothing of that kind."

She's gone, as well as the thoughts, but I expect
in heaven she is paying attention still.
It's a frail hope or merely an act of will
in the face of a reality I reject.

But I have seen for myself that paragon
of beauty and have encountered that rare soul
that all too soon returned to its proper sphere,

so I know that miracles happen even on
this earth and that they can transform the whole
of life whenever such passions appear.

296

I accused myself once, but I now excuse
and even take pride in how I lived in the jail
of my chaste body, suffering the travail
of a secret love that brought bruise after bruise.

The envious Fates destroyed the spindle that
spun the golden threads that bound me tight
and the golden arrow that was my delight
eager for death's release and requiescat.

What happy soul in love with light and laughter
would not change places with me for the true
joys of love, however much pain they bring.

I am content and shall be grateful hereafter
for every wound that I received from you
and the bondage in which I taught myself to sing.

297

The two mighty enemies made a truce:
Beauty and Chastity found a harmony
in her where they lived in peace and amity,
the bonds of which only Death could loose,

sundering them so that they are again at war.
One has returned to its home in paradise.
The other, here on earth, has covered those eyes
from which came the darts I was eager for.

Her wise and gentle speech, her graciousness,
and her sweet gaze that seemed unearthly then
have vanished, and I long to follow her,

but in the meanwhile, in the minds of men,
my wish is to memorialize and bless
her precious name as her biographer.

298

When I look back on those years that are now
gone forever and think of their raging fires
and freezing chills that came from my desires,
and those restless nights I suffered through somehow,

and when I consider how all I held dear
was taken from me and hidden in faraway places,
in heaven's purlieus and in the earth's embraces,
I ask myself how and why I continue here,

naked, alone, desperate, with others' pain
looking attractive compared to what I endure,
and I wail at Death, and Fortune, and my Fate

about that day when the illness and its cure
ruined me. Since that time, I remain
a shell of a man reduced to this low estate.

299

Where is that smooth forehead where any slight
change in expression could make or break my mood?
Where are those lovely eyes in which all good
seemed to dwell and were my guiding light?

And where are the words, the gentle gestures, the wise
counsel she always had to offer? Where
is that combination of beauty and virtue, so rare
in this broken world that its value magnifies?

That face, or even its shadow, could revive
my weary soul and prompt my finest thought,
but where is it now? Where has it gone? Why?

She held my life in her hand when she was alive,
but I, my life, and my world have come to naught.
She has gone, and my eyes will never be dry.

300

I look at the earth with jealousy because
it has in its embrace the one who is gone,
whose lovely face I used to look upon
and from all struggle find a blessed pause.

And heaven, too, I envy, for it holds
the spirit that is freed from its carapace,
and is at ease now in a better place,
a glory that a greater glory enfolds.

Those blessed souls I envy as well, for they
consort with her in a holy intimacy
I yearned for here on earth beyond all else.

But most I envy Death, who took her away,
extinguishing my life as well, but he
delays the tolling of my funeral bells.

301

O valley that resounds with the echoes of my
laments, and you, stream, whose waters rise
from the torrents of bitter tears that fall from my eyes,
you beasts that creep in the woods, you birds that fly,

and you, the balmy and temperate air I inhale,
warming it with my fervor, you greenswards, sweet
when she passed across you with her dainty feet
that have turned bitter as any dusty trail,

you all look much the same, but are different now
in my mind and eye, for my joy has turned to grief,
and you are where all my sorrows may be found—

She has gone elsewhere: what strikes me is how
that has disfigured each blade of grass, each leaf,
and it is as if you were her burial ground.

302

In thought I ascended somehow to the bright
precincts in which she for whom I yearned
now lives, nearly the same as she was but turned
a little more gentle, much to my delight.

She took my hand and told me, "Have no fear!
We shall be together again erelong,
and this time we'll be doing nothing wrong,
but innocent and happy in this third sphere.

"No human mind can understand the peace
in which we find ourselves. My only desire
is having you here with me, which is delayed."

She lets go of my hand; her sweet words cease.
The fires of my passion blaze up higher,
and, had I been able to, I would have stayed.

303

Love, you used to stroll with me in these
delightful scenes beside the crystal streams
and chat with me on a wide range of themes
beneath the shady canopy of the trees,

our companions in these hills and dales,
which are, I know, the usual pastoral setting
of such discourse—although I am not forgetting
how we would also speak of my travails;

and you, the nymphs and dryads of the place
who dwell on that grassy hillside and by the brook
and who welcomed us among you on these forays:

look at me now. You will not find a trace
of the happiness implacable Death took,
as is his habit. Nothing golden stays.

304

Love's worms gnawed my heart, and in my pain,
as the flames of desire burned in me, I roved
the wild hills and the valleys that I loved
where the footprints of a wild creature were plain

and I sang of the cruel treatment I had known,
but with lapses in my prosody and rhyme,
for my thoughts were all awhirl at that sad time—
and therefore I had to rely on passion alone.

The fire is dead now, and a marble marker
stands over it, but had it continued to burn
into old age, as I improved in art,

I could have achieved a style, richer and darker,
that I was then only beginning to learn,
the sweetness of which would have split stones apart.

305

Beautiful soul, loosed at last from the knot
that bound you to Nature, turn your thoughts to me
whom you left behind in the deepest misery
that I have at last admitted is my lot.

Your heart is freed of the old distrust that could
make your sweet face glower on bad days;
now, released from cares, you may turn your gaze
in my direction and wish me only good.

Peer at that rock where the Sorgue's waters rise,
and you will find me, wandering aimlessly,
clinging to thoughts of you while from my eyes

tears fall, but look away then, lest you be
troubled by any regrets. In the tranquil skies
take comfort in the mists of eternity.

306

That sun that guided my steps along the way
to heaven has sunk into the earth: a stone
marks the spot. And I am left alone
to try to follow, but I go astray

and roam the wooded hills, a beast in the wild,
sorrowful but feared, my eyes downcast,
exhausted, and afraid I may not last
as I search for the faintest traces of her mild

presence. Love, you are my sole comrade,
and I look to you to tell me where to go—
not to find her but places where she had

once walked—and follow the footprints I know
will lead me to her rather than to the sad
Stygian lakes and caverns down below.

307

I had thought to fly up into the air
(not by my own power but with the aid
of him who spreads my wings) and serenade
Love's bonds that Death will sooner or later tear.

I was too slow, too frail. Think of a weight
on a slender branch that deforms it and bends it over,
and I, too, was forced at last to discover
that one must accept his limited, mortal state.

No clever creature ever flew so high,
and surely not one with a leaden tongue
and awkward style. I realized it was my

good fortune to have seen her when I was young,
and that was a far grander flight than I
ever deserved—and to that thought I clung.

308

The one for whom I exchanged the Arno for
the Sorgue and sedulous riches for a free
poverty has completely eluded me,
and I hunger and thirst, always eager for more.

In vain have I hoped to capture her and suggest
her beauty to the ages; this I do
so that they may know and love her, too,
but I fall short, although I try my best.

Now and then, I presume to make a crude
sketch, noting the echoes of the praise
she deserves, but think of the multitude

of stars and constellations that are ablaze,
whirling in the sky, and how they elude
description although they dazzle and amaze.

309

The age of miracles has not ended: we
had one in our time that heaven deigned
to show us, but it could not be detained
here and returned to the higher empery.

Love set my tongue free to show to men
who had never seen her who and what she was,
and a thousand times I've gone to my desk because
he bade me and have worked with paper and pen.

But poetry does no good. It has its uses,
but it cannot demonstrate, let alone persuade,
especially where matters of Love are concerned.

It may even be that language itself traduces
the real world. No verses that I have made
suffice. From reading "fire," you are not burned.

310

Zephyrus blows in from the west to bring
green grass and wildflowers that seem to dance
to the birdcalls of the courtship and romance
that bless the year and celebrate the spring.

The storms of winter abate as Jove looks down
at his daughter Venus. The sky turns blue above
a world that is preoccupied with love.
What reason then for the father god to frown?

For me it is different altogether. I
look about and see the vacancy
Heaven made in my life and the world and sigh

at all the exuberant happiness I see,
in the woods and in the salons, too, and my
heart snarls with a wild beast's savagery.

311

The plaintive nightingale, while the world sleeps,
mourns his losses—mate, offspring, whatever
they are—and fills the sky with notes that never
fail to move us. Whoever hears him, weeps.

All through the night he comforts me with his
eloquent grieving. My fate is my fault, too,
for my foolish denial that Death could ever do
harm to one who was like the goddesses.

Optimists are easy to deceive,
but who could have imagined such bright eyes,
dark and lifeless, buried in the dirt?

Only slowly have I come to believe
how fate is harsh. It is hard to rationalize,
but nothing is too beautiful to be hurt.

312

Neither the twinkling stars high in the sky
nor the well-caulked ships crossing the tranquil sea,
nor knights in armor in noble company,
nor the sight in the woods of a deer that scampers by,

nor news that what I had hoped for has come to pass,
nor poems of wit and charm that show great style,
nor a bevy of ladies singing together while
a fountain plashes in the lush meadow grass,

nor any other pleasant thing can bring
joy to my heart that is with her interred
whose bright eyes were my source of light, my suns.

Life is unending pain, a wearisome thing
I hope will not last long. I'd have preferred
never to have seen her, even once.

313

The time has gone when I could live in the fires
of passion. The one I loved has passed away,
about whom I would write almost every day,
but the formerly diligent quill now retires.

The face is gone, and the eyes that pierced my heart,
which is also gone, have followed her elsewhere,
and what is left of me is a husk, a bare
shell of myself, a negligible part.

She took my spirit with her to the grave
and beyond that up to heaven with her where I
see her decked with laurel for chastity.

I am down here pretending to be brave
until we are together again and my
immortal life begins and I am free.

314

My mind saw trouble coming from the start
and even when times were good, it cautioned me
that this couldn't last and that eventually
I would be wretched and all would come apart.

Her gestures enchanted me, as did her speech,
her beauty, and her poise, but even so
my mind saw through this and predicted woe,
while I dismissed whatever it tried to teach.

How could I ignore those soulful eyes?
I knew that sooner or later they would close,
and I would lose all that mattered to me.

It is not surprising then, God knows,
but I have had a glimpse of paradise
that many try to imagine but few men see.

315

My time of green grass and blooming flowers
had withered, and the fires of passion that burned
unbearably hot had gradually turned
down as I declined in all my powers.

My darling enemy began to gain
confidence and, despite her earlier fears,
trusted in me so that, after many years
of failure, I knew joy instead of pain.

Together we had reached that high plateau
where Love and Chastity can co-exist
and she and I were on good terms also.

But Death, who is always Love's antagonist,
interrupted us with a thunderous *No*
and kidnapped my sweet co-equilibrist.

316

After so many battles the time had come
for peace or at least a truce, and I could see
happier prospects for both her and me
to benefit from the swing of the pendulum,

but one who levels all things interfered,
and, like a cloud that drifts away, she, too,
was carried off by an ill wind that blew
from an inauspicious quarter and disappeared.

She might have tarried. My whiskers had turned white,
and I could be civil and less importunate.
We could have smiled together about our past

and shared regrets we could reciprocate.
Now, with the benefit of Heaven's light
as she looks down we are reconciled at last.

317

Love has allowed me a safe harbor where
I am no longer troubled by winds and waves
of passion, for at last maturity saves
us all from vice. Now virtue is in the air.

She would have approved this loyalty,
calmer perhaps but not at all less true,
and over time this sweet affection grew,
until Death came and took her away from me.

Had she lived longer, I might have spoken to
her chaste ears and told her how, all along,
it was love that I felt in all its delicacy,

to which she might have answered that she knew,
and say that now it was no longer wrong
for her to admit that she also loved me.

318

A tree fell in the forest, uprooted by
a powerful wind. Its leaves spread out on the grass
and its pale roots in the bright sunshine, it was
a sad sight, I thought with a gentle sigh.

Another tree nearby stood straight and tall
with its roots in my heart (the muses sing of this
often as a figure of lasting bliss),
protected, secure as ivy that grows on a wall.

That was the living laurel in which my best
thoughts would come to roost and settle down.
Its leaves were never fluttered by my sighs.

Transplanted now to heaven's eternal rest,
it still draws nurture up to its living crown.
From its boughs a bird calls; no one replies.

319

Faster than deer my days have scampered and shied
into the shadows: whatever good I've seen
has gone in the blink of an eye: times that have been
sweet turned bitter because they did not abide.

The world is unstable and full of misery.
Whoever trusts in it must be mad or blind.
The one to whom I lost my heart, unkind,
it has reduced to dust and vacancy.

Her form, her idea, survives and will always live
in the heights of heaven, which makes me love her more
with a fixity that humans can seldom give.

Gray-haired now and feeble, I adore
her with the ardent if contemplative
certainty I always knew was in store.

320

I sense the old aura and see the light
that enlivens the hills where she was born and kept
me happy for a time until I wept
for her departure into eternal night.

O fleeting hopes, O jumbled thoughts, absurd
fancies . . . Even impassive grass is bereft
and the waters mourn for her remains that are left
in the cold ground in which she is interred

and where I also wish to be. Can I
imagine the comfort I might take if she
walked across the grave in which I lie?

Love was a cruel and stingy master: he
warmed himself by the blazing fire of my
passion that now is the ash of mortality.

321

Is this the nest where the fabulous phoenix would
don her dazzling plumage of purple and gold
and where, to protect and nurture it, she would hold
my beating heart under her wings? She could

draw forth sweet words and sighs from me and make
me glad, although I burned in the phoenix fire
in a pain that men would envy and admire.
She is in heaven now for her goodness' sake,

while I remain behind with my old pain
that brings me back here to honor the place
and take some solace in its familiar terrain.

Night comes on to demonstrate the grace
of your ascent, for the darkness in its train
was once made bright by the radiance of your face.

322

I shall never be able to look at your*
ingenious verses with a tranquil mind.
They're full of love and kindness, and I find
the impressive skill that you were admired for.

Earthly mourning could not overcome your brave
spirit that still pours down from heaven sweet
wisdom in elegant rhymes and intricate feet
in the wonderful stylishness you always gave.

I thought to show you a piece I did when I
was young and had just earned my laurel leaves,
but you were taken away too soon who were my

patron and teacher. But it is your friend who grieves
even as he praises you with a sigh
of regret, which is what simple emotion achieves.

---

* Giacomo Colonna. Petrarch here follows the rhyme scheme of one of
  Colonna's sonnets.

324*

Love, when hope for gain
for years of fidelity was running high,
she whom I had served was taken by

cruel Death. O cruel life, you leave
me in sorrow and pain
and kill my hopes before they could bear fruit,
and it is against my will that I remain
behind to mourn and grieve,
for Death will not permit my swift pursuit.

She is still here, if mute,
my Madonna, who dwells within my heart
and can inspect my life or this sad part.

---

* A ballata.

326

Cruel Death, the worst thing you could do
you have done, ruining the entire
realm of Love by quenching its sacred fire
and destroying its fairest flower, my Lady, who

lies in the earth. You have despoiled the lives
of all of us and of our ornaments
you have seized the finest and taken it hence.
But fame persists and courage always survives

in Heaven's brightness, which you cannot touch.
People will remember her always. She
is a novice angel, looking down on me

in pity, and she hears my desperate plea.
Let Death find me and in his bony clutch
take me away. My heart has been hurt too much.

327

The breezes, the delicate scents, the cool shade
of the laurels, the trees in bud and then in bloom,
the light of my life . . . Death put them in a tomb
who delights to unmake whatever heaven has made.

As the sun in an eclipse abruptly wanes,
so does my light, my life, and in despair
I entreat Death to come to me to repair
what he has done and end my lover's pains.

You have slept a short while to awake
among the blessed spirits where forever
you reunite with your maker in perfect bliss.

But if my rhymes have purpose, it is to make
your name live on among the wise and clever
eternally. My tributes are for this.

328

I can remember the last happy day
of which I've had but few in this short life.
I felt a premonition sharp as a knife
that the happiness I'd been given would not stay.

It was not unlike a fever's coming on,
the pulse wrong, the muscles weak, the mind
disturbed so that ideas of any kind
skittered away and into oblivion.

Her lovely eyes that day took leave of mine
to bring their joy to heaven but leave me
here, abandoned, battered, and supine.

But she intimated to me with certainty,
"Be at peace, dear friend: this is a sign
that we shall be reunited speedily."

329

Ah, the day, the hour, the instant when
the stars configured to impoverish me!
And your sad face! As if you knew I would be
from then on the unhappiest of men!

Now I see it, too. I thought I would
be losing only a part of myself in leaving.
But I understand it now, and I am grieving,
for my hopes have scattered like fallen leaves in a wood.

Heaven was opposed all along to my dreams
and doused the brilliant lights upon which my
life depended, which is to say her glances.

How was I supposed to know? It seems
I put a foot wrong somewhere and now I
find myself in ruinous circumstances.

330

That virtuous gaze of hers appeared to say,
"Remember this! Take what you can from me,
for never again on this earth will you see
your dear foe: I shall have moved away."

What is an intellect good for if not to give
some warning of impending catastrophe?
Had you looked at her face more scrupulously,
you might have seen the threat to how I live.

She seemed to say, "Heaven expects me now,
and He who first bound me unties the knot,
but yours will hold. Your stay is not so brief.

"Do not complain that it's unfair, for what
has that to do with the lives the Fates allow?
You will, alas, remain, as will your grief."

333

Go forth, sad rhymes, as a pilgrim might progress
to the cold stone that hides in the colder earth
whatever in my life was of any worth,
and call on her, who may look down and bless

us both, and tell her that I have long since
wearied of striving through these turbulent seas.
Say that I wander here under the trees
she walked among to follow in her footprints.

Report how we have spoken of her alive
and dead, or rather immortal, so that she
may be understood and loved by all,

and ask her to see how sadly I survive,
looking forward to death when we may be
united if I am graced by heaven's call.

334

If virtuous love is worthy and pity moves
merciful people still, then I shall find
mercy, because my faithful heart and mind
have shown the world the pattern of men's loves.

She used to fear me, but now she knows that I
want what I always wanted, which is a pure
love that never fades and is secure
unlike all carnal passions that soon die.

I hope, for all my sighs, we can be friends
in heaven—as it already seems we are,
for I feel her understanding and confidence.

When I've shed this husk and tried to make amends
for my imperfections, there may come a car
swinging low from Christ to bear me hence.

335

Among a thousand women I saw one
of such worth that I felt both love and fear
because she brought a celestial spirit here
to warm the earth as if she were the sun.

She had no taint of mere mortality
and that was why immediately I yearned
to be like her and with her, for I spurned
earthliness and ephemerality.

But she was too light and fine, while I was base
metal that melted in the refiner's fire,
and the thought of our differences now strikes me dumb.

I see her reigning in that glorious place
she has deserved and we long for and admire,
the impossible model for what we try to become.

336

She comes to mind (or in fact, stays there
for not even Lethe could erase her) the way
she was when I first saw her, bright as a ray
of a first-magnitude star and just as fair.

She is so chaste, so lovely and self-contained
that I cry out, "That's she! And alive still!"
and I beg her say a word to me if she will,
or if she would, or if somehow she deigned.

Sometimes she does, or seems to, but in my delight
I correct myself, as one must learn to do,
and tell myself it is merely a trick of the mind,

for in thirteen forty-eight, at the end of the night,
on April sixth, her blessed soul withdrew
from her body and the world of humankind.

337

Far sweeter than the perfumes of the east,
far brighter than the cultivated flowers
we grow in the west to decorate our bowers
and by which our rarefied pleasures may be increased,

is my laurel tree in the branches of which there were
all beauties, as well as virtues in its shade.
Love, my noble lord, sat in that glade,
the charms of which were characteristic of her.

In its crown my finest thoughts made nests
where they endured both biting cold and heat
and where in any weather I knew bliss.

It was too fine for earth, and now it rests
where God transplanted it up to his sweet
presence where its proper setting is.

338

O Death, you have left this world a black
and dismal place and robbed it of its sun;
Love is your captive, disarmed and undone;
Grace and Beauty have fled from your attack;

Courtesy is exiled; Chastity
is held in low esteem. I grieve alone
for everything of worth that is now gone
in desolation's total victory.

Earth, sky, and sea all ought to weep,
for mankind without her is like a field
stripped of its flowers, a ring without its gem.

Who knew her worth when she was here? I keep
her memory fresh since we have had to yield
her up to heaven to wear its diadem.

339

With Love's assistance I was able to see
her grace and beauty, but only the parts that were
mortal: I could not perceive the rest of her,
limited as I was by mortality.

To the best, the most of her, I was quite blind
or could not endure with my weak, earthly eyes
nor could I in my imagination surmise
virtues as rare as hers and as refined.

Nothing I wrote of her was anywhere near
adequate, but even so she repays
me with devout prayers in that higher sphere.

How could I look directly at the blaze
of the sun she was or describe it? It is a queer
fact: the brighter the light, the dimmer your gaze.

340

My precious pledge whom Nature took from me
and whom Heaven has in its keeping now,
I have begged for your pity and I ask how
it is so long delayed. How can this be?

You used to appear, if briefly, in my dreams,
but now you let me languish in my grief
without these simulacra of relief
in a scorn I thought that Heaven disesteems.

It happens down here that even the pious feed
on others' pain, and comradeship gives way
to self-absorption that can fail to heed

complaints of the afflicted. But people say
Heaven is different and better, and I need
at least to hope, and it is for this I pray.

341

The mischievous angel who carried her away
so prematurely did not have the last word,
for ever since that dismal event occurred,
my Lady's presence has contrived to stay

to soothe my grieving soul with such concern
that I can divert my ruminations from Death
and the wearisome exercise of drawing breath
to a kind of life to which I can return.

How blessed is it to lessen others' pain,
as she does in the apparitions I
am grateful for and I fall in love again.

"Be brave," she says. "I do not say good-bye,
for we shall reunite and I shall explain . . .
everything!" And in happiness, I sigh.

342

My lord provides great feasts of tears and sorrows
with which I feed my heart in its constant hunger.
Trembling, pale, I wonder how much longer
I can survive through all my grim tomorrows.

But she, who in life was such a paragon,
still visits my sickroom in charity,
speaks her sweet and soothing words to me,
and even sits on the bed that I lie on.

She has stroked my troubled brow with that same hand
I used to desire so much and spoken in sweet
words in which I drowned: "I understand

that knowledge by itself cannot defeat
anguish—and it is not a reprimand—
but live, for I live, too, in glory's seat."

343

When I remember the slight tilt of her head,
the sheen of her hair, the angelic voice in which
she spoke to me and gave my life such rich
moments, it turns my beating heart to lead.

How can I be alive? Without her aid,
I'd never survive, but she who offered me
the choice of whether truth or beauty be
the greater shows me that her spirit stayed.

She greets me with a smile and listens to
my litany of woes, which, as she hears
me speak, diminish as one's troubles do

in retrospect. But when the sun appears,
her precious image, fading from human view,
returns to heaven, her cheeks now wet with tears.

344

There must have been a time when love was not
bitter, but I cannot recall such days.
Even so, it still deserves our praise
as we discover, whether it's cold or hot.

I miss those pangs of suffering that she
occasioned before she left us for the heights
of heaven. I think of all those sleepless nights,
which continue even now to trouble me.

Death has stripped me of my earthly hoard
and that she thrives in heaven does me no
good, and I am not at all restored.

I weep and sing and carry on as though
nothing has changed. She whom I adored
has left me here behind in familiar woe.

345

Both Love and Grief had commandeered my tongue
to complain and say aloud what I ought to have kept
back, untruths, half-truths, and all the inept
strategies of writers when they are young.

Now she is beyond all that, and I
am relieved as well as consoled, for she is where
the blessed go, that heaven of which a share
was always in her heart to be guided by.

I am content that she is out of this hell
we call the world and would not wish for her
return. If I must live alone, ah well,

I'll do so, knowing that she is in a whirr
of beating wings of archangels who dwell
at the feet of the universal arbiter.

346

The chosen angels and all the blessed souls
surrounded her the day that she appeared
in heaven and were incalculably cheered
when her name was inscribed in their holy rolls.

One said, "What an amazing light is this!"
Another remarked, "Such spirits are most rare
that arrive this bright from the dismal blackness there."
Thus was she welcomed home to eternal bliss.

She is happy there, I'm sure, but still
in charity looks back to check on my
progress here and make sure that I will

follow her. And I am encouraged by
her generous wishes I hope to fulfill
as her prayers for me float down from the clear blue sky.

347

Ah, Lady, at last you reap the great reward
of a virtuous and deserving life and sit
in the Lord's presence on a high throne fit
for queens, adorned with jewels that none could afford.

From that lofty vantage point you see
my love and can bear witness to the true
faith that spilled so many tears for you
and so much ink for you in poetry.

You know that here on earth my heart was yours
as it still is in heaven and that I sought
nothing more than the sunlight of your eyes.

I may have been wrong during our long wars
to spurn the rest of the world as no one ought
to do—but it is through you that I grow wise.

348

Those amazing, limpid eyes, that gentle face,
the hair that shimmered as she moved and made
even the brilliance of golden sunshine fade,
the sweet speech and the smile that were full of grace,

those arms that could have vanquished all Love's great
rebels, even when they were in repose,
and the small and slender feet, the delicate toes
of a body only heaven could create,

these woke my spirit to life and now are gone
in heaven's precincts where the holy choirs
delight in them. I am bereft and blind.

In misery my mind is fixed upon
her soul the entire universe admires:
she is my hope, since I have been left behind.

349

Every hour, whispering in my ear,
I hear—or think I do—my Lady's sweet
voice, and my transformation is complete,
a diminution: I all but disappear.

My accustomed life I find it hard to recall,
and my focus is on when all this will end.
Laggard death has now become my friend
and I grow impatient as time seems to crawl.

I shall be happy to leave this prison where
all is wreckage, ruin, and debris
strewn about in failing light, for I

shall soon ascend through and beyond the air
to join my Lady who will welcome me
into heaven's mansion in the sky.

350

That wispy idea of beauty we all adore
made of wind and shadows will never appear
in a single body—or rarely, it can cohere
as it did in her one time and then no more.

Nature begrudges such gifts when the rest
are poor, but to demonstrate that it can be done
she lavished all her riches upon one,
the nonpareil, the paragon, the best.

Never before and, I fear, never again
was there or will there be an equal to
what she was, although the world took no

notice when she appeared for a moment and then
vanished. I was one of the fortunate few
who recognized on earth her heavenly glow.

351

A stern sweetness, the equanimity
of her refusals, her unflagging compassion,
and even her shows of anger that, in her fashion,
checked my burning importunity,

her speech, always courteous and refined,
and her modesty that was virtue itself in bloom,
and the fountainhead of beauty that left no room
for the base thoughts that arose in my troubled mind,

a gaze of such divinity that it blessed
anyone whom it noticed, edifying,
eliciting whatever in him was best,

and reviving his spirit that was sick to dying—
this was my salvation. All the rest
of my life was redeemed without my trying.

352

Oh, happy spirit that ruled those eyes and me,
striking my soul, eliciting my sighs!
She spoke words so loving and so wise
that echo still within my memory:

I saw you once shining with virtue's fire
walking among the violets and roses
as an angel might, in a series of graceful poses
that I shall always remember and admire.

You left that splendid body here in the earth
that cloaked it like a veil when you returned
to your Maker's realm as was your destiny.

Your departure occasioned a drastic dearth
of Love and Courtesy. The light that burned
in the sky dimmed to a dismal vacancy.

353

The nightingale can sing and at the same
time weep, declaring to the night
the griefs and losses of its poignant plight
that have prompted it so sadly to exclaim.

If it knew, in addition to its own
troubles, some of mine, it would surely fly
to me to console and to be consoled by
as we shared sigh for sigh and groan for groan.

Are we the same? The one you weep for may
still be alive. Death has been less than kind,
and the one I loved he has taken away.

But pain is pain to any troubled mind,
and happiness that time must always betray
is what we mourn together in ties that bind.

354

Lord Love, reach out your hand to help my lame
and tired style speak of her who is
a citizen of a better realm than this,
for I am in despair and full of shame.

Help my words to soar, as they cannot do
on their own, to fly up to reach the heights
of beauty, virtue, and such other delights
as in this world we're not accustomed to.

Love answers, "It's not me you need but her
whom Death took from us. She was your inspiration
with the chaste beauty she is remembered by,

equaled by none since Adam met Lucifer.
in Eden. In tears I relate this information
that you already know as well as I."

355

O time, whirling along as the stars turn
that leave us mortals dumbstruck, sad, and blind;
O days, as fast as arrows and as unkind!
Your deceits have taken years for me to learn.

But as Nature gave you wings, she gave me eyes
that I could use to observe what caused me pain
not merely sharp but shameful to explain
(but only from its teaching do we grow wise).

It is long past the time to turn these woes
to another and better direction. I do not reject
Love's yoke but my own grievous faults: for those

the change will take great effort, I expect,
as Love, my implacable master, surely knows—
but it is my life to ruin or perfect.

356

My breeze that bears her name arrives at night
to whisper in my sleep and embolden me
to confess my pains quite unashamedly
as I never could when she lived in the light.

I tell her of that first glance of hers that struck
the spark that flamed within me and began
the years of exquisite torment no one can
imagine unless he's had the same good luck.

She does not respond to me, but her gentle face
is full of pity. She sighs, and sometimes tears
spill down her cheeks. My soul is swept away

in my chagrin. I am grateful for the grace
she shows me now after all those years.
Chastened, I wake to face another day.

357

Each day drags on, a millennium I must
contrive to endure until I can at last
follow my beloved guide who passed
on, leaving me here in the world of dust.

This life's delusions cannot hold me here.
I know them all and long since have learned
where true happiness lies, and I have turned
toward Heaven from which the light is bright and clear.

Nor do I fear death's threats, innocuous
when I think how our Lord endured far worse
to help all mankind and do good for us.

My Lady blazed the way: I am not averse
to following in her felicitous
footsteps, taking heart that they are hers.

358

Death cannot disfigure her lovely face,
which can make Death's own grim visage pleasing.
She is my guide and constant comfort, easing
my way through earthly perils by her grace.

And He who saved us with his precious blood
and forthwith harrowed hell provides me strength
to carry my lighter cross until, at length,
Death summons me as I have hoped he would

without delay. My time has surely run,
but that was the case the moment that she left
this life—I haven't truly lived since then.

I have no purpose anymore but the one
hope of joining her. I am bereft
and only in death can I find life again.

361

My candid mirror tells me clearly, and my
weary spirit agrees, and my sagging skin
and diminished strength proclaim the state I'm in:
"You have grown old, and soon you are going to die.

"Nature cannot be denied but will
have her way, and you cannot resist."
It becomes clear then, looming out of the mist,
what I must come to, a bit further down the hill.

Our lives fly by: too soon we arrive at this
and realize our allotted time is gone.
Is there another life? No one can say.

She may now be secure in heaven's bliss,
who in her life was such a paragon,
but I am blessed to have known her, either way.

362

I visit heaven so often in my mind
that I begin to feel I belong with those
blessed souls who left the earth and rose
to another life, perfected and refined.

I fancy I hear the one I love tell me,
"You have changed your habits as well as your hair,
and I am pleased with you, dear friend, and care
that you should find reward in eternity."

She leads me to her Lord, before whom I
kneel and beg that he will let me stay.
I look at them both, beseeching and entreating.

He says, "The thirty years will soon go by,
which seems long to you, but is like a day
to us. And I promise you will then have your meeting."

363

Death has extinguished my sun so that my eyes,
however healthy they may appear, are blind
or say that they see a blackness that is refined
to blot out familiar objects under the skies.

The laurels, oaks, and slender elms that grow
were pleasant once but now cause only pain,
and my thoughts are enough to poison hill and plain,
infecting every landscape with my woe.

Love stabs and heals, but I have escaped his grip
and have found an uneasy freedom from his wiles,
though not through any virtue or scholarship.

The Lord in heaven has put an end to my trials,
and his peace is the object of the trip
I shall conclude after a few more miles.

365

I was weeping and moping, in love with earthliness,
and therefore never learned to soar in flight.
I had wings that I never put to their right
use, a grievous fault I now confess.

You can see all my defects, Heavenly King,
and can mend my soul, in tatters now and frayed.
Having been indifferent and having strayed,
your mercy is the hope to which I cling.

I have lived through struggles and storms but now
wish to die in safe harbor, at peace.
My life has been unruly, I will allow,

but I am much improved. Let my decease
be graced and graceful. Put your hand on my brow,
and yours will be the praise at my obsequies.